FIRST CHURCH
OF THE
HIGHER ELEVATIONS

Mountains, Prayer, and Presence

FIRST CHURCH
OF THE
HIGHER ELEVATIONS

Mountains, Prayer, and Presence

PETER ANDERSON

CONUN
DRUM
PRESS

AN IMPRINT OF BOWER HOUSE

DENVER

Printed in Canada.

ISBN: 978-1-942280-17-0
Library of Congress Control Number: 2014958613

10 9 8 7 6 5 4 3 2

For Grace

Contents

Foreword

by Paul Lacey

WHAT DO MOUNTAINS, PRAYER, AND PRESENCE HAVE TO DO WITH one another? We go to the mountains for grandeur of perspective that takes us out of ourselves by showing us the infinite expanse of nature to which we belong. We go for the aesthetic pleasure of wildness, to escape from humans and human works. We go for solitude, to risk living with only our own company and thoughts. We go for challenge, to pit our strength against hardship, adversity, and deprivation. We go to recollect ourselves, to explore, to find our way home. And we go to encounter the Divine.

Peter Anderson's book touches on all the rich complexity of what he calls variously "the scripture of place," "the geography of the heart," "the landscape of the imagination," and "the topography of memory." We can learn a great deal here about mountains and how to center and walk and climb in prayer, but he has not created a "how to" book. Instead, he shows us his own practice and offers "trail notes" of actual journeys–road trips across the Great Plains, sojourns at the Earlham School of Religion, seasonal work as a wilderness ranger with the U.S.

Forest Service, long solo treks and companionable walks with his wife and daughter.

The book has a clear trajectory. It begins with Recollection, goes on to Exploration, and concludes in Home Ground. Another way of seeing its shape is that the book starts with "Ground of Being" and ends on "Home Ground," an extended meditation which breaks open the catch-all phrase "homeland security" to reflect on its constituent parts: home, land, and security. But we don't have to stay on the beaten path, for Anderson invites us to go off the track, to double back over familiar ground and savor the accumulated experiences of many trips. Some sections are like toprographic maps, others like medieval maps to the Holy Land that figure the heart's longing more than correct distances. There are even some quick back-of-the-envelope sketches of the way home.

This book *explores*–a word which literally means "to cry out"– and it implores–a word which means "to pray," but literally means "crying in." I am reminded that St. John of the Cross gives us two interconnected prose works to explicate his inner quest: *The Ascent of Mount Carmel* and *The Dark Night of the Soul*. Ascent and descent, inward and outward, dark abyss before celestial light. Peter Anderson tells us he has two longings–for a dwelling place of the Spirit and for the terrain in which to ground it. This sends me back to Paul Tillich, whose description of God as "the creative and abysmal ground of being" glosses so much of Peter Anderson's accounts of "the Big Empty," terrifying vastness, the hovering dangers of wildness, peril from armed fugitives, cabin fever, deadness and despair which poison solitude.

But that makes First Church of the Higher Elevation sound far too dark and serious. It is also joyous and funny. Peter Anderson is a good companion on a climb, with a lot of resources in his pack. His companions include John Muir, Jack Kerouac, Thomas

Merton, Han Shan, Douglas Steere, Gary Snyder, Carl Jung, Wendell Berry, his wife Grace and daughter Rosalea, as well as Jimi Hendrix, Jerry Garcia, John Coltrane, and B.B. King. Sometimes the wilderness rocks. Sometimes there is beer in the cooler.

What does a book about mountains, prayer, and presence offer an aging, sedentary flatlander like me? Certainly it calls up my own recollections of the very different landscapes where I have met the Divine. Some books do that for us, telling us about unfamiliar things, allowing us to imagine ourselves into their reality. Some books explore an outer world so as to give us metaphors for our common inner world. So I put down Peter's book to go find Gerard Manley Hopkins's poem "No worst, there is none" and read again the lines

> O the mind, mind has mountains; cliffs of fall
> Frightful, sheer, no-man-fathomed. Hold them cheap
> May who ne'er hung there.

And I briefly recover my companionship with Hopkins through my companionship with Anderson.

"The elusive summit," Peter tells us, "is an apt symbol for the longing that gives shape to the lives of seekers and mountaineers alike." Whether or not we climb physical mountains, this book will help us traverse the heights and depths of the inner terrain and know that ground of being where we are most at home.

Paul A. Lacey is Emeritus Professor of English at Earlham College, author of The Inner War: Forms and Themes in Recent American Poetry, *and* Growing Into Goodness: Essays on Quaker Education. *He edited the poet Denise Levertov's posthumous volume* This Great Unknowing: Last Poems *and her* Selected Poems. *He also served as Chair of the Board of Directors of the American Friends Service Committee.*

Introduction: Revisiting First Church of the Higher Elevations

IT'S BEEN ALMOST TWENTY-FIVE YEARS SINCE THE QUERIES THAT LED to this book first surfaced in the pages of what was then a daily journaling practice. What is the relationship between place and prayer? How might prayer affect one's sense of place? What do mountains have to do with the life of the spirit?

I was living in Salt Lake City at the time, attending Quaker meeting on Sundays and walking the foothills of the Wasatch Range most every morning, often before the sun came up. And I was trying hard to make sense of periodic bouts with "the black dog" of depression and the solace that I found, that I had always found, in wild places. As a city dweller at that time, I looked for and found that solace on the edges of our urban home, in the foothills of the Wasatch Range, and I found it in the High Uinta Wilderness where I worked as a seasonal wilderness ranger. I also found it in the fluent silence of Quaker Meeting, which led me to believe that the inward stillness, even liberation, I felt in meeting was somehow akin to those walkabout experiences in the higher elevations.

Wildness, as I understand it, is a self-sustaining dimension of life beyond the confines of human control. Encountered outwardly in a place or inwardly in contemplative practice, it has been an opening, centering, and healing force in my life. Wilderness is a place where natural systems are left largely untrammeled. Similarly, there are deeper dimensions of self beyond the controlling ego, the ego which poet Gary Snyder describes as living "in a little cubicle near the gate" that opens into wildness. Beyond that gate, one's inward ecology takes care of itself. This is the soul's equivalent of a wild place. It was a place I knew best inwardly when I was able to be still.

Attending Earlham School of Religion (ESR), a Quaker seminary in Indiana, offered me an opportunity to try and understand how contemplative experience and the way of the mountain leads one into this kind of wildness. So I began with what I already knew from reading books like Kerouac's *Dharma Bums*, which I revisit in an early chapter of this book. Coming home to the West, I also sought out various "first church" practitioners including Trappist monks I knew at a monastery in northern Utah and an accomplished explorer, mountaineer, Jesuit priest, mentor, and my father's first cousin, whom I met in Santa Fe. But the transformative power of wildness isn't limited to any class, culture, or religious orientation. It is instead a widely experienced encounter described in almost every major wisdom tradition.

It seemed to me then, as it does now, that anything that nudges us toward wholeness is in some way holy. And wholeness, for me back then, had a lot to do with shaking off the black dog and learning how to feel alive again. ESR offered me a scholarship, a place to understand my attraction to the contemplative way as practiced by Quakers, and a supportive community where I could write this book. It was a good place for an extended period of recollection, during which I retraced a meandering trail of the

Spirit, wondering what it was about wildness that left me feeling so renewed. I equated that renewal with the experience of feeling at home in my own skin. I also knew it was bigger than that.

For four years beginning in 1996, I drove across the Great Plains twice a year: east, at the end of the summer, to begin another year of study at ESR; west at the end of spring semester to head home to Colorado. Over time, I came to think of these seasonal road trips as part of a cyclical movement between two longings: one for a dwelling place in the Spirit and one for a place in which to ground it.

Now, almost fifteen years after choosing a home here on the western edge of the Sangre de Cristo Range in southern Colorado, after twenty-plus years of marriage, after more than a decade of guiding my daughters (Rosalea, now fourteen; Caroline ten) through the early stages of their lives, I am rereading the book I began to write back then and finally finished here in the shadow of a mountain called Challenger. This process is akin to the kind of recollection that led to the book in the first place.

My old friend and mentor Paul Lacey used to emphasize three questions in his freshman humanities classes: *What do you know? How do you know it? So what?* What I know now, as I reread this book, is that I don't know much about anything as vast as creation, nor can I say much about any Force or forces that may guide it forward. The word "God" is at best a symbol of what we can never really name. As theologian Elizabeth Johnson wisely says, "All good symbols of God drive toward their own transcendence," which leaves me wondering how any mention of "the Big G" is very helpful anymore. It's too easy to get mired down in our own stories, which the word "God" only seems to encourage.

What I also know is that given some silence, stillness, and a healthy dose of wildness, I can do some deep listening. And if

I'm attentive, I may feel a nudge, some subtle guidance toward this or that choice, which in the end leaves me better off than I would have been otherwise. Quakers refer to the Inward Teacher, language that fits my experience, but with which I travel gently, since I also understand silence as the best way forward in discerning any truth. My experience of inward guidance might best be likened to the words of poet Rainer Rilke's words which turn up later in this book: "A gesture waves us on, answering our own wave,/but what we feel is the wind in our faces."

In recent years, I have come to believe that silence and the stillness it invites isn't just a quality of experience, but may itself be the very Presence that seekers like me want to know. It invites a spaciousness of soul, something that I came to understand in this book as the Big Empty. The Big Empty is a way of naming geographical space, but I think of it too as that inward spaciousness which, as Gerald May put it, "we may experience as open possibility or void nothingness; as creative potential or dulling boredom; as quiet peaceful serenity or as restless yearning for fulfillment." Interestingly, these same qualities of experience are also part of living here on the edge of a village at the end of the road.

Experiences of home, land, and security are never static here or anywhere else, nor are they ever fully grasped. They evolve as we do. Where that leaves the United States in its never-ending quest for "homeland security" is anybody's guess. George W. Bush, in initiating the "war on terror," once pledged to "smoke the gophers out of their holes." These days some say our pursuit of terrorists is like a global game of whack-a-mole. Either way, it wouldn't hurt to revisit the meaning of the words home-land-security, which is what I tried to do in the last chapter of this book.

The stories that follow focus on experiences of inward and outward wildness; some are my own, some I found, and some are told by those I met along the way. They all support an argument for the goodness of geographical and contemplative wildness. I hope they offer good company, good cheer, and maybe even a few laughs, to those who seek, or have found, some solace in the "First Church of the Higher Elevations."

—Peter Anderson

Part One: Recollection

Ground of Being

LATE IN THE SUMMER OF 1997, MY WIFE GRACE AND I WERE WELL into another Great Plains crossing. This time we were traveling in tandem: Grace driving the car that she would use to commute to her own graduate program in landscape architecture, while I followed behind in a truck and camper loaded with clothes, boxes of books, a banjo, a guitar, a genial Newfy-shepard mix of a dog named Willy, and Cleo, an especially skittish Siamese cat. I was following Grace across the darkened heartlands toward Salina, Kansas, where we had agreed to stop for dinner.

On that long road, with Jerry Garcia's guitar leads winging like barn swallows around the eaves of old-but-good *American Beauty* tunes, August lightning flashed around the hole in a Great Plains storm. Driving under the stars that were shining though a break in the clouds, I thought we might make it all the way to Missouri that night. But the clouds bellied over and sheets of rain were soon washing across the wipers, streaking the red left behind by Grace's taillights, and bending the white beams cast by an improbable electric cross off to the south of the highway.

Out on that dark and empty stretch of road, I drove by a lone exit sign. "Vespers," it said. I imagined white-robed monks, the lit cross spilling light into an otherwise dark chapel, with the wind gusting through the mesh of the window screens and into their chanted psalms. "If I knew the way, I would take you home," Garcia sang, as the last of that white light rippled across the passenger side mirror and lay down behind the rising prairie.

"Did you see that cross back there?" I asked Grace over dinner at a truck stop in Salina.

"What cross?" she wondered, only now able to uncurl her hands after a white-knuckled, hydroplaning drive through that heavy rain. I described the electric cross that I had seen. She listened skeptically.

The image of that cross lighting the dark prairie would stay with me—across the rest of Kansas, Missouri, Illinois, and into the first day of worship back at ESR in Richmond, Indiana. Why? Traditional religious symbols were not especially significant in the stripped-down, almost Zen-like style of silent Quaker worship where I felt most at home. Worship, as I knew it, was an inwardly focused practice devoid of anything resembling high-church images or liturgy. So it wasn't the cross alone to which I was responding. It had more to do with that confluence of light and night and prairie. It had more to do with that holy symbol, as I imagined it, anyway, embedded in the dark earth.

One of my intentions in going to seminary was to explore the relationship between place and Spirit. During our sojourn at ESR, we lived on the edge of a farm in southeastern Indiana. Beeches and maples, and a smell like vinegar when their wet leaves layered the ground, reminded me of autumns growing up on the east coast. Rural county roads and farm field skies were more reminiscent of the west where most of my adult life had been spent.

Before first light, I often walked the edge of a circular alfalfa field. The Big Dipper hovered over the small glacial mound that defined the western horizon where fields of corn met forests of oak and hickory, which fell away toward the Whitewater River.

Canada geese would be stirring near the neighbor's pond on the far side of those fields, right about the time my dog and walking partner passed me on the usual bend of our early morning path. I watched him bounding ahead, his back legs stiffened and barely able to keep up with his front, sniffing the air for the white-tailed deer whose silhouettes we often saw out ahead of us at that time of day. On that circle that we walked each morning, my intention was to listen . . . to open myself, as best I could, to that moment and that place. In my thoughts, I carried a few words from John's gospel: "Make your home in me, as I make mine in you."

The spiritual education and refuge that we sought out at ESR puzzled many of our friends out west. "No matter how you change out there, we'll still be friends," said one of my old mountain buddies, as if I would return, knocking on his door all moon-eyed, arms full of religious tracts.

Like us, most of the friends we made at seminary were seekers, many of them in one form of life transition or another, all of them looking for a way to live a life that was rooted more deeply in the Spirit. But few had logged much time in the mountains of the Southwest—the First Church of the Higher Elevations—where Grace and I were most at home. That was to be expected at a seminary in the Midwest. So was the yearning we felt, from time to time, for the geography we had left behind.

Grace, a lifelong westerner, was feeling an especially strong sense of exile in the Midwest. One night she dreamt that she had discovered a new mountain range in southern Indiana. That was right about the time I had rediscovered an interest in the *Rand McNally Road Atlas*, map-gazing wild lands west of the Great Plains and scouring the Indiana map for geographical diversions. I happened to notice, one day, that we were about twenty miles away from the highest point in Indiana.

I found the highest point in Indiana on the edge of a corn field, not unlike all the other corn fields I had passed on this drive-about to the north and east of Richmond. I walked a two-rutted trail along the edge of the field, climbed the steps of a stile up and over a barbed wire fence and entered a forest clearing surrounded by oaks, maples and shag-bark hickory. There I found several benches, a sign identifying this place as the highest point in Indiana, and a register inviting me to sign in and comment. More than a few high land wayfarers had logged in, some of whom had made a covenant to visit the highest point in all fifty states. "Today Indiana, tomorrow Illinois," said one.

"Upward. Onward. Excelsior," I wrote as I added my name to the register. Humble high point though this may have been, it still invited a moment or two of reflection. I thought of the great ice sheets that had once come down from the north and scoured this land. And I imagined a drop of water, finding its way down south, through the hills and rills and hollows into the Ohio River Valley.

Why the attraction to high places? Why climb a mountain? For the same reason that one seeks that restful center or stillpoint in prayer, which Dante likened to an inward summit. Mountaineer George Mallory put it simply: you climb a mountain because it's there. Anything short of "there" leaves climbers, and wayward souls alike, forever restless.

Reading of psychologist Carl Jung's inward and outward explorations further illuminated the relationship between mountains and prayer and the longing I felt for both. Having grown up in the Alps, Jung encountered mountains early on in his life. At the age of fourteen, his father took him, by cog railway, up a mountain named the Rigi:

> With tremendous puffing, the wonderful locomotive
> shook and rattled me up to the dizzy heights where ever
> new abysses and panoramas opened out before my gaze,

until at last I stood in the strange thin air, looking into the unimaginable distance . . . I kept carefully to the paths for there were tremendous precipices all around. It was all very solemn, and I felt one had to be polite and silent up here, for one was in God's world. Here it was physically present. This was the most precious gift my father had ever given me.

For the rest of his life, especially during times of great stress and fatigue, Jung would return to the mountains, either by foot or by way of the imagination. After decades of exploring the inscapes of the soul, he would come to understand the mountain not only as a symbol of "pilgrimage and ascent," but also as a symbol of "the Self." Conscious awareness was only part of this wider and deeper strata of the self. If there was an inward summit where one could listen for the holy whisperings of the Spirit, it was in the untrammeled ground of one's being where it would be found.

Another story I was drawn to at seminary spoke to the tension between that which one finds on the mountain and that which one has to leave behind. Luke's gospel describes an event known as the transfiguration this way: "Jesus took with him Peter and John and James, and went up on the mountain to pray. And while he was praying, the appearance of his face changed, and his clothes became dazzling white." That Jesus' face changed didn't suggest anything supernatural. But when coupled with the Greek word that described Jesus' clothing as "dazzling," a word also used to describe a flash of lightning, Luke's description suggested that Jesus was seen in the midst of an extraordinary light.

"He was transfigured before them," Matthew's gospel says, "and his face shone like the sun." Though Peter, John and James had been "weighed down with sleep," they were now fully awakened, dazzled by the glory of what they had just seen. Peter didn't want to leave the mountain. Why not build a couple of dwellings there, he suggested? But this was not to be. An extraordinary moment of relatedness with the moment, with that place, and most of all with Jesus, had come and gone. Peter couldn't stay on the mountain of the transfiguration any more than he could remain in that illuminated moment. Still, I could relate to his desire to do so.

And I could relate to Jesus' yearning to return to the mountains, time and again, for periods of contemplative renewal. After the feeding of the five thousand, after a day of teaching in the temple, after healing the man with the withered hand on the Sabbath, "he went out to the mountain to pray."

In the Episcopal church where I took my first communion— all the while wondering how and when the Holy Spirit would turn up in the midst of it all—I probably heard about Jesus on the mountain, but it would have been lost on me. Back then, I had no experience in which to hold those words.

Some years later in 1974, I was a college freshman taking a southwest studies course based in Santa Fe. One evening, word came by phone that my roommate's brother had been killed in a car wreck back in Illinois. It would be another couple of hours before his redeye flight would be leaving Albuquerque. How best to spend the time?

We knew intuitively that we had to get out of the dorm where we were staying, so I drove my roommate and another friend into the foothills of the Sangre de Cristos. I remember the three of us hugging for a while in that chilled October breeze that carried the smell of piñon, juniper, and sage. And I remember my roommate wandering off by himself and leaving at least some of his grief in those foothills.

I don't remember praying that night. What I remember was a sense that I had done right by my friend . . . that walking those hills, with the dark outline of the high Sangres and that great starry space encompassing it all, was in itself a form of prayer. This may be a strange notion of prayer to some. But it is less strange in a region where place names like Sangre de Cristo evoke the confluence of place and Spirit. And it is less strange when prayer is understood, in its contemplative form, as a way of emptying, opening, receiving, and giving thanks.

Trail Notes:
Hesperus Peak

HOW DOES PLACE AFFECT ONE'S SENSE OF THE SPIRIT? HOW DOES prayer affect one's sense of place? What can mountains teach us about the geography of the heart? I bring these queries east across the Great Plains and into my work at seminary. And they lead me into an extended period of recollection—one in which I want to revisit some of the mountain people and places that prompted these queries in the first place.

That Hesperus Peak comes to mind is no great surprise.

On summer breaks from seminary, which we spend with Grace's family in southwestern Colorado, Hesperus, the highest peak in the La Plata Range, is the pinnacle of our summer climbs. It is a classic mountain ascent—through spruce-fir forest and alpine meadows filled with wildflowers, up the long gradual pitch of a tundra-covered ridge, around a few cliff faces, and on toward a boulder that appears to mark the summit, but which in fact is only a precursor to the resting place and lunch stop that still lies beyond our view.

Navajos say that First Man and First Woman emerged from a hole in the earth, bringing soil from the world below with which they shaped this mountain. Into a pile of this soil, First Man added pieces of a shiny black gemstone called jet. Then he shaped this mountain which is known to the Navaho as Dibe Ntsaa, the black mountain of the north. He fastened it to the earth with a rainbow and covered it with darkness. Every twelve years, Navajo healers return to these mountains to replenish the soil in their prayer bundles. Home ground, in a very real sense, is where their prayers begin.

I walk respectfully on Dibe Ntsaa, knowing that it is a sacred place for the Navajo. But for me it is no more sacred than Moss or Spiller or any number of peaks in the La Platas. As much as I might admire the Navajo story, I don't live in it as I might if I had heard it from my elders.

What stories then do I bring to this mountain? And how do they influence my experience? I know there is something for me here in rock and light, in that sensation of being at the center of this great dome of sky. On this summit—looking north into the tangle of high peaks that make up the San Juans, west to an island of a mountain called the Sleeping Ute, which rests on the high desert beyond Mesa Verde, south to a volcanic outcrop called Shiprock that floats in heat waves rising over Navajo country, and east into the rest of the La Plata Range, I know where I stand. Along with the geographical clarity that comes with elevation gain, I sense a new orientation in my being. In a few lucid moments, it is as if the boundary that defines my sense of "self" has become more permeable. I feel less contained, less isolated, and more like a moving part in a greater entity called mountain, called Hesperus, called Dibe Ntsaa.

On the summit of Hesperus, I take a notepad register out of an old peanut butter jar and read the words of those who have been here before me. Susan, from Littleton, Colorado, filed this report: "This makes number four for me today—Babcock, East

Peak, Lavendar, Moss, and here [isn't that five?] . . . time to go down and take a nap." Two days later, Bill logged in with this comment: "Get it Susan," followed by Ron a week later: "Susan is an animal."

Dennis's entry qualifies as an epic. "Awesome! Broke both bones above ankle five years ago . . . three and one half years in a leg cast . . . two and one quarter year on crutches. Five major reconstructive surgeries—last one last year at this time. I made it!!! Hope I can get back down. P.S. Rock n' Roll forever."

"Otter" and "Rabbit" have logged in, as have "Kachina" and "Katie the Wonder Dog," some of the four-leggeds making the ascent. We hear from Bob, a fledgling mountaineer: ". . . spilled water on clothes in pack. Cold. 2nd peak ever." And, as always, there's an ode to food: "Awesome day! Can't wait to get down to Mancos for some ribs at the Millwood."

Some mountain travelers like to keep it short—"Yahoo!" or "Hi World!"—always punctuating with exclamation points. Some writers stick with the facts: "winds > 35 knots, gusts of 45 . . . intermittent snow and hail." Others wax melodramatic: "In the mountains I am home . . . And yet I am alone. No one to love . . . Ed, Salt Lake City."

Testimonies are ecumenical. Denise offers a jumbled up line from a poem by St. Francis: "Thank you mother earth, brother moon, sister sun." Andy has been listening to the sound of one hand clapping: "The higher you get, the higher you get." Josh says: "I need to be a mountain monk." Comments like these are common in mountaintop registers, suggesting that the link between spirit and place is more commonly experienced than it is easily named.

The way back from the summit drops down by way of several long tongues of remnant snow into a broad cirque known as Owen Basin. The snow is soft and granular, but not soft enough to fall through. These are good conditions for a glissade—a long, slow boot-heel slide—but the pitch is steep enough to require a turn or two and there are enough rocks poking up through the snow to demand a little precision.

Sometimes there is nothing better than a hint of danger to call one home to a piece of ground in the moment. I pause at the top of this snow chute to imagine my route—just a brief foray into the future. Then I bend my knees, point my toes down the hill, nudge myself into the fall line, and gravity does the rest. I twist my knees and hips one way and then the other, feeling the forgiving texture of corn snow through the soles of my boots as I ride this slope down to the edge of the alpine basin below me.

From there, I drop down across the snowfield, hearing the headwaters of the Mancos River trickling down beneath early summer remnants of last winter's snow and ice. This is where the South Fork of the Mancos River begins. Farther downstream, it cuts a canyon where I pass by the ruins of a few old mining cabins. As I pay my respects at this memorial to the society of prospecting transients, I am reminded of an old timer named Bud who used to fill in at the trading post back in St. Elmo, an old ghost town near the Continental Divide where I once lived.

Bud had seen his share of hard times. He had a face that was as weathered as badlands shale. Once, he told me, he was so hard up for a drink, he broke a liquor store window and ran off with a bottle, only to find out that it was an empty display prop. Jail sobered him up and he had been dry ever since. A quieter life in the higher elevations did him good, he said.

I would visit with him over coffee, occasionally bumming one of his long and skinny extra-millimeter cigs. One morning, we got to talking and he told me he'd been up around Hancock doing some prospecting. He said he'd been up there most of the night.

"You were prospecting at night?"

"Yeah," he said. "I go up there in my sleep . . . it's kind of like flying. Sorta like Superman, only slower. I just fly around and look over the country. Sometimes I don't want to wake up."

Bud had taken me by surprise a time or two. Once he'd turned up at the annual St. Elmo Fire Protection Association's Fourth of July picnic dressed in drag, firing six-shooters into the sky, and nary a drop had he drunk. But astral projection? Or in Bud's case, astral prospecting? I could claim to have lost track of my soul in the Lariat Saloon a time or two, but as far as I knew, it had never taken flight. Still, I took some pleasure in imagining old Bud out there, hovering over Hancock, looking for traces of "color" in the rocks and streambeds below.

The act of recollection, of hovering over the topography of memory and seeking out those traces of Light that point the way toward a lasting sense of home, is a necessary piece of prospecting for wayfarers and transients both. Or so it seems to me, as I begin to consider again the experiences, which have been cairns along this trail of the Spirit.

First Church of the Higher Elevations

THE DHARMA BUMS, JACK KEROUAC'S VEILED ACCOUNT OF HIS TRAVels with poet Gary Snyder in the High Sierra, was the first book I can recall reading that suggested a relationship between mountains and the life of the Spirit. And it was one that seemed especially relevant when I first came west to live in 1974.

Like Ray Smith, Jack Kerouac's narrator in *The Dharma Bums*, I was a wide-eyed easterner, dazzled by the Milky-Wayed world I was able to walk into with a sturdy pack, a tent, and a warm sleeping bag. This wasn't the washed out suburban sky I had grown up with on the north shore of Long Island. Out west, as my grandfather once said of a night spent in the hinterlands of Texas, "the stars were so close, you could knock 'em down with a stick." Between those stars, the dark went deep.

Under that same wide sky, carrying everything he needed on his back, Ray Smith followed a sandy wash into desert mountains west of the El Paso freight yards. A sky full of stars and a slender moon lit his way as he began to gain elevation. Here, beyond the world of other railroad bums and the yard cops who were always on the lookout for them, he felt safe. "I got back to my camp and spread the sleeping bag," Smith said, "and thanked the Lord for all He was giving me." Then he prayed and meditated in a silence "so intense that you could hear your own blood roar in your ears . . . Louder than that by far [was] the mysterious roar . . . of silence itself."

I didn't know much about prayer or meditation when I first came west, but it didn't take long to catch the drift of that silence Kerouac had described. For three years I was a student at Colorado College. Pikes Peak was a dominant presence on that Front Range campus, but it was the territory on the far side of the mountain that called to me the most.

In May of 1978, I drove 24 West out of Colorado Springs, beyond Pikes Peak and over Wilkerson Pass, where the sky opened out into the windswept vistas of South Park and where distant peaks were gathering early summer snow on the Great Divide horizon; farther west and flat out down a long straight two-lane, stopping for beer and chips at the Hartsel Trading Post; farther west, riding the long curves up to Trout Creek, and coasting down the short ones on the far side of the pass; farther west, dropping into the Arkansas River Valley, rolling to a stop just past the Dinner Bell Cafe, and peering up through six thousand feet of clear mountain air at rocks and snow and the east face of Mt. Princeton.

The road to St. Elmo ran up the gap that Chalk Creek had notched between the shoulders of Princeton and Antero, another fourteen thousand foot peak a little farther to the south. It ran west from the Nathrop General Store and Post Office, following the grade of the long defunct Denver and South Park Railroad into the mouth of Chalk Creek Canyon. I drove it for the first time early one summer morning. I had just taken a job guiding trips on the Arkansas River and I had heard talk of a cabin for rent somewhere up the canyon.

The road turned to dirt as it began the steep climb along a stretch of the Chalk Creek Cascades, a half-mile of tumbling creek water—nothing but white at the peak of the run-off. Above the Cascades, ponderosa territory gave way to the higher grounds of lodgepole pine. The road swerved past aspens bent low by an avalanche the previous winter, past the first stands of Englemann spruce and subalpine fir, past the concrete remains of the Pawnee Gold and Silver Mill. As the road began to level out, it rounded a curve and the forest opened out into an unexpected alpine valley.

Straddling Chalk Creek, which ran down the middle of this valley, was this remnant of a town called St. Elmo. I drove slowly past the abandoned false fronts—the Miner's Exchange, Pat Hurley's Saloon, and the Home Comfort Hotel—spun a U-turn and pulled up next to the trading post, the only building in town that appeared to be in use. Walking the remains of a wooden sidewalk, I looked through the gaps between sheets of rusted tin roofing that covered up first floor windows. Most intriguing of all was the Home Comfort Hotel, where shafts of light revealed a floor strewn with envelopes, old brown bottles, and a pile of women's lace-up shoes. Morning sun glancing off the second story, drew my eye to the lace curtains, yellowed and torn, behind the slightly bent lens of century old window glass.

Pathos lingered, as it often does in a boom town gone bust, but St. Elmo was anything but gloomy that day. I crossed the bridge over Chalk Creek. A water ousel dipped and bobbed on a rock below me and flew off down the creek. The current swept up flashes of sun as it ran down through the willows. I walked over to a schoolhouse which looked as though it had received a fresh coat of white paint in the not-too-distant past, and sat down on the steps.

To the east were the ridges running down the back sides of

Mts. Princeton and Antero; to the south, beyond the old railroad grade, the stony cone-shaped peak of Mt. Mamma; to the west, the road to Tincup Pass and the Continental Divide. An occasional breeze stirred the aspens. Time, or at least my thoughts as I experienced them in time, swirled slowly here. And an inward space seemed to open that was as quiet and as welcoming as Ray Smith's camp above El Paso.

If it was wanderlust that got me to St. Elmo, it was an intuitive sense of belonging there that lured me into staying. Back in the old days, if a gold field played out, there were more out yonder. For Kerouac's religious wanderers, the yondering call had more to do with a geography of the spirit. And the paydirt had something to do with silence.

For Han Shan, a Japanese hermit and wandering monk, who preferred the slopes of a mountain to the monasteries in the valley below, "silence was the golden mountain." For Ray Smith and his mountaineering buddy Japhy Ryder, the words Han Shan left on the cliffs of Cold Mountain a thousand years ago were invitations into an openness of spirit.

Any comfort the orthodoxies of the 1950s may have offered in a post-holocaust, post-atomic bomb, cold war era, were not enough for the restless seekers Kerouac wrote about in *On the Road* and *The Dharma Bums*. They hadn't given up on the holy as much as they had given up on lifeless religion. For them, vital spirituality had more to do with adventure than security. To say that "silence was the golden mountain" implied that contemplation was a worthy destination and that a mountain path might help one get there.

So Ray Smith was looking forward to his first season as a fire lookout on Desolation Peak in the North Cascades. He was longing for the solitude that came with the job. "You're sayin' that now but you'll change your tune soon enough," said the wrangler who was packing him in and who had seen more than a few lookouts come and go. "They all talk brave. But then you get to talkin' to yourself. That ain't so bad but don't start *answerin'* yourself, son."

Settling into my first winter in St. Elmo after a season of guiding, hoping to complete a long piece of writing, the last of my college requirements, I imagined Ray as a kindred spirit. Though I didn't realize it at the time, I too was a little naive as I entered into my first winter of solitude.

At 10,013 feet, the storms came hard and fast. The cabin was at the end of the line for the county snowplow. With the nearest neighbor a couple of miles down the mountain, knowing that the plow would eventually show up offered some consolation when the big storms hunkered down on the Divide and the road down valley disappeared under a foot or two of snow. Still, cabin fever turned out to be more of a challenge than I had anticipated.

Back in the old days, miners faced the same storms in a boarding house near timberline—at least a thousand feet higher than my perch on the edge of St. Elmo. The remains of the Mary Murphy boarding house, still visible on a mountain south of town, prompted my curiosity. Who had worked there? What did they do between those dark shifts inside of Chrysolite Mountain? How did they weather out the long winter?

G.W. McPherson, a parson from back east, was a misfit in the mining culture of the Mary Murphy bunkhouse. Atypical though he may have been as a minister in a gold and silver camp, his sentiments on the mining life at timberline were likely shared by many, if not most, of his fellow miners. "It was lonesome as death far up on the Mary Murphy Silver mine," McPherson wrote,

the only sound being heard was the almost constant thumping of the persistent winds on the bunkhouse and shaft shed with an occasional dim, low echo of the [train] whistles . . . far away near the top of the mountain.

Compared to the Mary Murphy Mine and bunkhouse, downtown St. Elmo seemed downright suburban, even though I was the only full-time resident there that winter. Still, on a Sunday night in January, the silence at road's end could chill a heart as fast as it could fill one. It was often easier to stay for another draft at the Lariat Saloon down valley than it was to follow the dark road home. At times the sky behind the stars seemed so dark and so vast as I pulled up to the cabin that it was just plain overpowering. I'd slam the truck door just to break the silence, hustle into the cabin, throw the light on, and stoke the fire.

Reflecting on a summit experience in the Swiss Alps, an early twentieth century mountaineer named Emile Javelle described the sensation of an "emptiness, terrifying in its vastness," that opened out around him. One "is struck," he said, "as in no other place, by this thought that the universe is terrible in its mystery, that no religion, no philosophy, can give us a true idea of what it is; that the further the vision of our eye extends, the greater does that mystery become."

That experience of mountain vastness, especially for a newcomer to it as I was back then, was surely enough to get a guy talking to himself, maybe even answering his own questions. But the refuge and finitude of that one room cabin, with the stove throwing out a little light and heat, reassured me that I could handle a temporary overload of fear and wonder—that quality of experience we used to call *awe* before everything became *awesome* and the word lost its edge.

The mountain night at the end of the road was both compelling and unsettling, as were the worst of the winter storms that came down off the Continental Divide. Although town was an

hour or so down a slick and snowy canyon road, its amenities,
even if only imagined, offered some diversion on those days
and nights when the weather was leaning in hard on those cabin
walls. But that kind of meditation could be hazardous.

One storm, which showed little evidence of letting up after
dumping several feet of snow, taught me a lesson or two about
waiting. I gave into my own restlessness and paid the price when
I ran the truck off the road and into a ditch down valley. "Just
cause you got four wheels spinnin' don't mean you can go anywhere," said the guy who towed me out.

With time, I got better at waiting. After the storm clouds began
to lift, after the plow driver had come in for coffee and gone back
down the mountain, my best mountain and river buddy from
Leadville would eventually come rolling up the road. After layers
of wool, after boots and gaitors and the Dillards singing "What's
Time to a Hog?" on the boom box, after packs were loaded up
and skis were waxed, came the first kick and glide tracks on the
old railroad grade to Hancock. All was quiet, save for the swish
of skis on fresh powder—maybe the occasional chatter of chickadee, gray jay, or squirrel. Now and then, a gust of wind would
loosen a branch load of snow from a nearby spruce.

By mid-day, we were ten miles up grade, slicing salami and
cheese next to the remains of the last old cabin in Hancock. This
had been the hermit's stomping ground. Frank Gimlett, prospector, poet, and recalcitrant recluse, had once run jack trains
in this neck of the woods:

> Well I remember the blizzards of the '80s when we would
> just get a trail shoveled out and another storm would
> come up the same day, and only by superhuman effort
> and continuous work, were we able to get the train of
> jackasses over Chalk Creek Pass and down to Hancock

town. Then it took sledgehammers to break loose the ore sacks from saddles, while great icicles were hanging from the faithful eyebrows and whiskers of the old beasts. Many times it was already very late in the day, and to make any attempt to return and go back over the trail to Middle Fork would be just plain suicide, so we stabled the jackasses in the barn for the night, while we made up a bed of saddle-blankets in the corner and there on a couch of new hay we rested, and what I mean, slept through the night.

The Hermit of Arbor Villa, as Gimlett was later known, lingered long after the glory days of the mining era had come and gone. In his later years, he lived in a cabin ten miles or so to the south of Hancock. In the pamphlets he wrote and printed as an old man, his voice was at once ornery and sentimental. When he wasn't pining away for a lost love, or waxing nostalgic for the life of the prospector he had known working the highline between Garfield and St. Elmo, he was cursing Grover Cleveland's decision to replace gold and silver money with paper—the ruin of the mining west, as he saw it. He was in love with a past that had slipped through his sluice box and run down the creek.

On those days when we skied past the old Hancock townsite, and on those winter nights when we pitched camp a mile or two farther up the old railroad grade toward the Divide, his hermit stories lingered. Saddleblankets in a warmed barn full of hay sounded pretty fine compared to insulite pads, polarguard sleeping bags, a frost-filled tent and the likely prospect of frozen boots in the morning. But there were many moments of gratitude as the winter night came on: for squeaking fresh snow underfoot, for a pot of macaroni and cheese, for a cup of something hot (better yet hot and spiked), for the telling of stories under Orion and the Pleiades and that Milky Way canopy.

One day, we crossed Hancock Pass, a few miles south of our camp. On the Hermit's old highline trail, we were able to walk up a low windblown saddle. On the far side, we stepped back onto our skis and scoped out the run. Later, it was almost as satisfying to retrace those long "S" turns looking up from the bottom of the pass as it had been to make them on the way down. Though more transient than even that prospecting hermit, we were at least present enough to savor those moments that the wind would soon cover over. In the First Church of the Higher Elevations, which was something, I imagined, like Han Shan's golden mountain, the moment was the sacrament. And the double helix lines we left in the snow, like the little gratitudes that came with winter camp, were all a part of the liturgy.

Like those days in St. Elmo, Ray Smith's hitch in the North Cascades would eventually come to an end. Shortly after Smith heard on the radio that his first full season as a fire lookout would soon be over, he acknowledged days passed and vision gained: "Sixty sunsets had I seen revolve on that perpendicular hill. The vision of the freedom of eternity was mine forever."

What exactly was this vision he was talking about? What did he mean by the freedom of eternity? What he was describing were transitions from *chronos,* or clock time, into *kairos,* a time that can't be measured. To experience kairos time was to experience a fullness in the moment. It was as if a two-dimensional world momentarily opened out into three dimensions and then, in a flash, reverted back. One was left with the fleeting impression that there was a deeper and wider way of experiencing the world.

Hints of that experience seemed to come and go as Ray strad-dled the geography where his Buddhist orientation met his Christian roots. Aspiring bodhissatva that he was, I heard him reaching out in meditation: "I called Han Shan in the mountains:

there was no answer. I called Han Shan in the morning fog: silence, it said." Aware of his aloneness in that silence, he took solace in the warmth of the passing moment: "Mists blew by, I closed my eyes, the stove did the talking."

It was easy enough to forget such moments . . . to let them slide into the past without recognition or acknowledgment. And yet those moments of being present were potentially moments of opening up to Presence. Ray Smith left Desolation Peak behind, but he took something with him as well. I heard him naming a fullness of heart that had grown out of those contemplative moments: "I have fallen in love with you God," he said on the way down the mountain. "Take care of us all, one way or the other."

Though I understood the emotion underneath Ray Smith's prayer, I can't say as I had fallen in love with God after that first winter in St. Elmo. Back in those days, Saturday night was still my Sabbath. Much as I might have been drawn to silence and solitude, I wasn't about to miss Saturday night at the Lariat, the "Rope" as we called it, when the Lazy Alien Blues Band was in town. In that hot and smoky swing dance of a mountain town scene, with the boys on the horns blasting out the riffs to "Midnight Hour" or "Land of a Thousand Dances," the Lariat would be shaking. Crack a brew, fire up a smoke. Wild night was calling.

Back then, the notion of long term commitment was as abstract as prayer. Still, I had imagined that I was ready to make that kind commitment to my adopted home—that Chalk Creek and the Arkansas River were the watersheds to which I would pledge my allegiance, as Gary Snyder had suggested. For another six years or so, I cobbled together a life in St. Elmo and the Arkansas Valley—guiding river trips, banging nails, and later taking a job as reporter for the *Mountain Mail* (Salida's five-day daily) covering northern Chaffee County—everything from town council meetings in Buena Vista to the crowning of the rodeo queen.

But as it turned out, my time there was only a courtship. In the early 1980s, dreams projected onto the *Rand McNally Road Atlas* were as seductive as word of a new placer strike once had been. This was especially true when there were layoffs at the molybdenum mine in Leadville, downtown store fronts were emptied in Buena Vista and Salida, winter winds were frosting over the windows at the Lariat, and good friends were firming up their plans to move elsewhere.

Many friends had bailed out of the Arkansas River Valley. Even my best mountain and river pal, who had weathered a few booms and busts living up in Leadville, was soon to be California-bound. I found myself heading into town more often and settling in at the Lariat. "Buck up," I imagined the old Hermit saying, but I knew that I'd be leaving before the aspens turned again.

You can't store much in a one-room cabin, which is a good thing when it's time to move on. Most of what I owned—tools, camping gear, river stuff, skis, clothes and books—I could fit into the back of a truck that had become a kind of camper shell Conestoga. Whatever didn't fit wasn't needed.

It was harder to leave the intangibles behind. I wasn't sure what to do with that deep welcoming, unlike any I could recall, that I'd sensed in that little valley at the head of Chalk Creek Canyon. Nor was I sure what to do with the uneasiness I'd known in the dead of that winter solitude. But I took along a pinch of dust from Ray and Japhy's golden mountain, ever grateful for a shack and for the silence at the high end of the road.

Trail Notes: Four Corners

I LEFT THE ARKANSAS VALLEY IN 1985 AND ENDED UP LIVING FOR A
while in Durango, a lively mountain town in southwestern Colorado. As a stringer for the *Denver Post*, I wrote feature stories.
Periodically, I would pitch story ideas to the State Desk and more
often than not they were interested. So I was able to range freely
around southwestern Colorado and occasionally into Utah, writing the kind of features I enjoyed—relieved to have left the part
of my old beat that included school board and town council
meetings. One story idea led me out to Alan Neskahi's powwow
south of Cortez and into an experience of prayer that would
nudge me further along on the trail of the Spirit.

In addition to putting on an annual powwow, Alan had dedi-
cated his home, also known as the Spirit-Life Center, to a ministry
that melded Navajo tradition with the teachings of Christianity.
Like his father before him, Alan was a circuit-riding evangelist
of sorts, ministering to makeshift gatherings on the "rez." Back
in the summer of 1986, I arrived at his door thinking that he
would be a great profile story. With reporter's pad and camera
close at hand, I sat down on the couch in his living room. Alan
settled his burly frame into a well-worn easy chair. Grandchil-
dren played at his feet. His wife and daughter spoke quietly over

coffee at the kitchen table. He wasn't a man to be rushed into anything, nor was he inclined toward formality. He was more interested in talking about an upcoming powwow than he was in talking about himself.

"You oughta come out to the powwow this weekend," he said. I muttered something about not wanting to intrude.

"All people have their place . . . just like the four directions and the four colors," he said. "We come together to share out here. You oughta come out . . . maybe you'll find something."

That weekend, I drove out south of Cortez, less interested in writing a story and more interested in just being present. I arrived at Neskahi's well before the sun had come up over the La Platas in order to join an early morning "sweat" that began each day of the powwow. Even though I had no reason to feel anything but welcome out at the Neskahis—I knew that Alan's invitation had been sincere—I felt self-conscious as I walked out through the still empty cottonwood arbor that surrounded the dancing area, worried, I suppose, that I would land myself in a crowd of gawking white spectators, or worse, starry-eyed Indian wanna-be's.

Right around daybreak, I met a couple of Alan's sons who came home every year to help out with the powwow.

Out by the bent-willow sweat lodge that stood beyond the arbor, beyond the arroyo, beyond the tall clumps of sage, and beside a cool stream of water that ran through an irrigation ditch, they were lighting a fire with a rolled up newspaper. "If this were a real traditional sweat," Arly said, "we'd be lighting this with the *Navaho Times*."

"Building this fire is like a guy tying his own noose," said Chuck, an Anglo friend who had become something of a regular out at the Neskahis. Meanwhile Art Neskahi pitchforked hunks of lavarock into the flames. It wasn't until the rocks had been taken into the sweat lodge and a canvas flap had sealed us in darkness that I began to feel that noose.

Eight of us sat in a circle around those rocks. Art splashed them with a ladle of water, which hissed into steam. My lungs ached. I bent over to shield my face, gasping for air until I had the common sense to hunker down, face forward into my lap, as close as I could get to the dirt floor where the heat was less intense. I tried to mop the sweat off of my forehead with a bundled clump of sage before it poured down into my eyes. Then came more water and another wave of hissing steam. In that dark heat, even a long-delinquent Episcopalian like myself could find reason to pray.

As with any sweat lodge, this canvas-covered dome had been intended as a place for prayer. It took me a while to realize how the heat had focused my attention in such a visceral way, on each breath, on each drink of water, on each song, on each prayer. In that dark heat, I heard songs whose notes would have flown off the scales in any hymnal. And I heard words spoken that could have come right out of *The Book of Common Prayer*.

Art later told me that the sweat lodge was a place where he had been able to honor his own Navajo tradition along with the teachings of Christianity. In the darkness that day, his prayers had indeed embodied the spirit as well as the language of both traditions.

For a day or two afterwards, I would notice the faint smell of the sage that had been baked into my pores. And that would remind me of dirt and sweat, of rock and water, of dark and light, of one breath and then another . . . sacraments that had grounded me. And like the sage, the essence of the prayers and songs we shared would linger somehow long after I had gone home to Durango, along with a vague reassurance that something like the Holy Spirit was alive and well.

I kept going back to Neskahi's. Once a month, we'd catch word that Art was going to run a sweat. About a half dozen people, Navajos and Anglos, would gather out by the fire. Taking swigs of water from plastic jugs, we watched the flames and made light of the fact that we would soon be basting in the dark. Some months later, a few days before I left to begin a graduate program at the University of Wyoming, I joined the other "sweathogs," as we had come to call ourselves, for one last experience of heat, prayer, and fellowship.

"When the wind whips through Laramie," said one of my friends afterwards, "think of us down here sweating in the dark." I did think of them. Often. Never before had I experienced a form of shared worship with that much spiritual voltage. Nor had I sensed the kind of vulnerability that I heard expressed in that dark heat.

Art eventually grew weary of running the sweat. He began to find more sustenance in the Native American church. No one else could sustain that curious blend of traditions that had offered a kind of temporary shelter for a few wayfaring souls.

A few years later, I would follow the lead of an old sweat lodge friend into the prayerful silence of Quaker meeting. But it was in that dark heat out at Neskahi's that my interest in prayer began to grow. And it was in that dark heat that I began to understand prayer as a way into the center, the inward summit—that "little plot," as Dante put it, "for which we wax so fierce."

The Contours of Worship

IN THE SALT LAKE VALLEY WHERE I LIVED FOR SIX YEARS DURING THE early 1990s, mountain topography and temperature differentials often trapped the clouds during the winter months. For weeks on end, we saw little of the sun in our neighborhood on the northern edge of the city. But the foothills of the Wasatch were just up the street. And there were times when a little elevation gain was enough to free us from the heavy gray light of the inversion.

So too there were times when walking prayer was enough to lift, at least momentarily, an inversion that had hidden the horizons in that big thicket of thoughts, emotions, and memories that I had come to think of as an inward landscape. If it seemed as though mountain walking and prayer were somehow complementary to one another, it was also true that the lifting of that which obscured the "inward light" was as complex and mysterious to me as the interplay of elements that carried the low clouds of an inversion up and over the Wasatch Range.

I knew from the Bible there was precedent for the experience of renewal that I came, over time, to associate with walking, prayer, and higher ground. On a mountain, Moses saw the burning bush. Elijah heard that still small voice. Jesus was transfigured. Mountains were often regarded as the geographical edge or ecotone where divinity and humanity encountered one another.

In a similar way, the silence of Quaker meeting had become for me an inward edge where I occasionally felt graced by the fluent stillness I found there. As on the mountain, there were no barbed-wire fences or "Keep Out" signs in the geography of silence. On first visits to the Salt Lake Meeting, no one told me what to think or how to pray or what to do as I sat there in the silence. In that inward landscape, there were no paved trails or brochures. Newcomers were simply welcomed into the openness and darkness of the silence and given the opportunity to find their own way. There were books and pamphlets and Quaker 101 classes that would be helpful later on. And there were those who had mapped the inward territories as they had experienced them, who would serve as useful guides. But for the most part, orienting oneself and finding a way in the geography of silence was best left to the individual and the guidance of the Spirit.

In meeting, the medium of communion was a stillness found in silence, not unlike the stillness one often finds above timberline. Ideally, the stillness became a kind of shared "inscape" in which one opened oneself to a Holy Presence. Sometimes words spoken in one heart had also been heard in another. And even when there weren't any words spoken at all, one might leave the meeting with the experience of having heard or of having been heard in the midst of that fluent silence.

In Quaker worship, as in mountain travel, one left the usual routine behind. A seasoned traveler paid attention to the movement of the Spirit, much as a mountaineer might notice a shift in the wind or the movement of the clouds. On the mountain, as in worship, there were forces at work that were far more powerful than one's own desire or will. George Fox, whose mystical preaching back in the mid-1600s first gathered seekers into the Religious Society of Friends (Quakers), knew this to be true.

Early on in his life, he had struggled with a sense of worthlessness. "I cannot declare the misery I was in, it was so great and heavy upon me," he said, trying to describe the dark moods that oppressed him. In his journal, he wrote of various attempts to "look for comfort." The clergymen he sought, one of whom he described as "an empty hollow cask," were "miserable comforters." He went to a physician for help but the physician misdiagnosed the problem and prescribed a course of bleedings, leaving Fox "dried up with sorrows, grief, and troubles." Other people, he finally realized, would not heal his malaise. Better, he figured, to read scripture, to fast, and to listen for the breath of the Holy Spirit in the winds that blew across the Peak District where he often went walking.

On a foggy day back in May of 1652, George Fox's highland wanderings led him up the flanks of Pendle Hill which, at 1,830 feet, was a substantial piece of rock in that part of England. As he gained a little elevation, the clouds were thinning and he began to see patches of blue. By the time he reached the summit, the wind had scattered the clouds. Awash in the light of that winnowed sky, moved, as he put it, to "sound the day of the Lord," he let loose a howl that seemed to carry off, at least for a while, the malaise with which he had been struggling.

I had never taken to fasting. And I knew I would never come close to being as steeped in scripture as Fox was (he had memorized most of the Bible). But I understood Fox's struggles with "a sense of his own worthlessness" and his "temptations to despair." Those experiences were not unlike those that I had come to know in periodic bouts with depression. Fox's story left me feeling a little less isolated. He struck me as a fellow traveler. When the light of healing eluded him elsewhere, he too lit out for the territory. For me, the "territory" began any place on the map where road lines broke off, contours ran tight, and elevation numbers promised the kind of higher ground that I often sought out on a ridge above our urban neighborhood.

On the pre-dawn saunters my wife Grace and I took above our Salt Lake City neighborhood, I had no intention of "sounding the day of the Lord" in the manner of George Fox, but I was open to walking in prayer. As we followed the winding furrows of an old jeep trail up a foothill draw and onto open ground, Grace and I would often share our "joys and concerns," as they say in the small town church where we were married. On other mornings we kept to ourselves, climbing quietly toward first light.

On days when my "concerns" were embedded in a recurring internal monologue all but emptied of hope, breaking the silence was of little use. It was better to walk and breathe and listen for the sweet song of the lazuli bunting, if I could listen to anything at all.

Winding up through that first ravine full of magpies and towhees and scrub oaks, leaving behind the latest wave of new luxury homes that were steadily carving into the flanks of the foothills, we rose up over the bench which had once been the shoreline of an ancient lake that covered much of the Great Basin.

From the top of the knoll, we walked out into the eerie night-wash of city-glow. Like green grass in stadium light, the soft browns and tans of the wide slopes between us and the ridgeline above were ratcheted up a few shades too bright to look entirely real. The thin layer of haze that hung over the valley bent symmetrical streetlight rays of blue, red, green, yellow, and white until they shimmered. Below lay the great grid of the Mormon Mecca, illuminated arteries bisecting the rectangular blocks that Brigham Young had laid out so meticulously.

Looking down on this valley I had chosen as home, my eyes were often drawn to the lights of the temple. On top of a temple cupola, a bronzed Latter-Day angel named Moroni beckoned believers to the center of the Mormon world. This was the city, according to Mormon belief, that would one day be taken up into the heavenly realm.

I wasn't drawn to speculation, Mormon or otherwise, about the "heavenly realm." Though I appreciated the good-hearted sincerity of the black-jacketed, white-shirted Mormon missionaries who came by to knock on my door every now and then, their words did not speak to me. But their homeland did.

On some of those early morning foothill climbs, I walked casting two shadows. The smaller of the two was a silhouette blotting out a body's worth of light cast by a West Desert moon bound for Nevada. The other was an elongated shadow cast by city light that crept up the ridge toward the hazy stars of Cassiopeia.

In the cityscape below me, I imagined a 7-11 clerk at the end of his night shift, leaning up against the counter, unwrapping a cheese Danish and reading about the Jazz on the sports page of the *Tribune*. Southeast a few blocks at Bill and Nada's, one of the regulars would be jingling a spoon inside an empty coffee cup to get the waitress's attention. Over in the willows beside the Jordan River, someone living in a cardboard shack would be waking up to the sound of the Union Pacific freight train whistle we would hear some mornings from the top of the ridge.

Often we heard a great horned owl hoot as the train whistle faded. In the margin between grid glow and the darkness of the north slope, city light spilled over the crest of the ridge and dissipated, as did the remnant snow banks that tapered off into clumps of oak that rose up out of the canyon shadows. Deer shuffled through the oak leaves. Coyotes and porcupines occasionally appeared then disappeared, headed for cover.

Shortcutting the curve of the ridgeline in front of us, we crossed patches of remnant snow on the north slope, ice crystals flashing moonbeams up from the hardened crust of wave-like drifts. We walked in the imprints someone else had made a day or two earlier, digging hands into the crust upslope on the steeper pitches. Back up on the wind-worn crest of the ridge, we followed the exposed ruts of a trail carved out by the tires of renegade four-wheelers. On toward the still-distant summit, morning stars grew dim in the yellowing sky.

On a ridge only a little less steep than this one, a wild gait and a shortness of breath once revealed my lack of mountain experience. Eyes riveted to the top of a pass, I was more interested in the destination than I was in the process of getting there. An older mountaineer took notice and offered some simple, yet sage advice. "As the slope gets steeper," he said, "shorten your steps. When you take a step, take a breath. And when you take the next step, let it go . . . ."

When I practiced that technique properly, climbing became a kind of moving stasis: the oxygen coming in fueled a slow and steady burn instead of an energy inferno. If I could stay focused, I was rewarded with the energy to get to the top of the pass and beyond.

It would be a few more years before I would learn to appreciate the stillness in the midst of that motion and many more before it would occur to me that climbing and prayer both opened trails into a less constricted interior. On those early morning Wasatch walks, I began to carry a word or a phrase in thought, something I had heard spoken out of the silence at meeting, or a passage that had lingered from the Quaker writers I'd been reading.

I knew that some people had the spiritual discipline to pray ceaselessly in a jail cell or in a kitchen washing dishes and I knew that I wasn't one of them. But as the ridge turned steep on the final approach toward the summit of that foothill peak, I was forced to pay attention to that step and breath rhythm without which I would have quickly come to a windless standstill. I tried to wrap each breath around a few words—two syllables for every inhale, two for every exhale: *"Be still . . . and know . . . that I . . . am God."*

On the circumference of my vision, looking to the south I could see Olympus, Timpanogas, Mt. Nebo, and other snow-capped Wasatch Peaks. The Oquirrh Range and the Stansbury Mountains, the first crests of the rocky waves and troughs that made up the Basin and Range country, defined the horizon as I looked out toward the dry side of the valley. Beyond the tip of the foothill spur on which we walked, bare rock islands floated like holy land hallucinations in this dead sea desert. Rimming the eastern edge of the Great Salt Lake, stretching north to Ogden and beyond were the marshes and wetlands and bird refuges. Between the lake and the spine of the Wasatch Range headed north, was a geographical alleyway between mountain and lake for migrating songbirds, as well as sixteen wheelers on the interstate, who were only passing through.

As space opened out near the high point of our walk, so too, from time to time, an inward way seemed to open, much as I had come to experience in the silence at the Meeting House. I don't mean to suggest that a cluttered mind cleared in that instant of topping out. Just as it had taken many steps and many breaths to gain a few thousand feet over our Salt Lake neighborhood, it had taken many moments of prayer to empty myself enough to feel as though there was a longer pause between my thoughts.

There were days when I found only a fleeting relief on the mountain, when the descent was the inverse of the ascent. Like the night-blooming primrose we passed on that foothill ridge, any opening I experienced on the way to the summit would fold in on itself as the brightness of the morning came on. In the rising tremor of morning traffic, chest muscles pulled taut.

Lungs were emptied of Wasatch air.

Descent was especially disheartening on days when the inversion seemed to have settled in for good. There was some solace in knowing that only a thousand feet up, I could walk into cleaner air, not to mention a little sun and sky. But each foothill ascent through that layer of cloud and the subsequent descent back into the gray miasma deepened my longing for a break in the weather.

Still, an occasional glimpse of sky was enough to remind me that nothing stayed the same. As a thought, that was nothing new. But to feel this fact, to know it internally, was often a significant shift, much like any movement in the clouds that hovered over the valley.

On the day when an inversion finally began to lift, the light that came streaming down across the high snowfields of the Wasatch would surely melt a little of whatever needed thawing. So too, in some small way, did those early morning ascents onto that foothill ridge. Or so it seemed as I let the contours of that slope shape my steps, and followed the prayers that I carried in one breath and then another, up the ridge toward the summit.

The sheltered spot behind a boulder where I would wait for Grace to catch up wasn't exactly a summit. It was one of several high points on a ridgeline that ran straight and treeless, except for an occasional scattering of firs and pines and curl-leaf mountain mahogany, before it dipped down into a saddle and curved around to a higher peak at the head of City Creek Canyon. It wasn't the high point on that long crescent of a ridge, but it was a good place to watch the light as it streamed through the craggy peaks to my east, falling first on the high ridge of the Oquirrh Mountains along the far western edge of the valley, then down their scrub oak flanks, slowly sweeping up the shadows of the Wasatch that lay across the city. As in meeting for worship and walking prayer, it was a place to dwell, for a moment or two, in the Light of a day's slow turning.

Trail Notes: Abbey of the Holy Trinity

IN A BOOK CALLED *THE WATERS OF SILOE*, THOMAS MERTON described the founding members of the Abbey of the Holy Trinity as a "solid nucleus of veteran monks and lay brothers" from Gesthemane, his home monastery in Kentucky. On July 7, 1947, this "body of select men, vigorous, happy, already steeped in the . . . contemplative spirit," boarded a train bound for some high altitude ranch land in Utah. On July 10, they rode up the same canyon road east of Ogden, gaining almost one thousand feet in elevation.

Their train rumbled east across this valley, which Merton described as "rugged and austere and simple . . . stripped of nonessentials . . . with no irrelevant details to arrest the eye." It seemed well suited to a group of monks intent on creating a no-frills farming community centered on a life of prayer. But as Merton pointed out, "transforming this desolate, houseless ranch into a . . . monastery and farm would be an immense amount of work."

Saint Benedict, a sixth century Italian abbot who wrote *The Rule of St. Benedict* on which Trappist communities like the Abbey were based, believed that work was a way of sharing in the ecstasy and agony of God's creation. "Thy kingdom come, thy will be done" was the implicit prayer in every ditch dug, in every garden grown, in every meal prepared.

This wasn't always easy. "Monastic work is often hidden, humble, anonymous, even monotonous," wrote Father Charles Cummings, one of the monks at the abbey who had become for me a friend and mentor. "The human ego resists hiddenness and prefers the achievement of tangible results, the more spectacular the better."

Given the prospect of hacking down weeds with Father Joseph, one of the original monks who had come out west from Gesthemane, I wasn't expecting spectacular results. I wanted only to give back a little to this mountain place and this community where I periodically sought out quiet refuge from the busy-ness of an urban life in Salt Lake City, writing and teaching English at a community college. In a month or so, I would be headed into the backcountry of the High Uintas, an unusual east-west trending mountain range on the Utah-Wyoming border, where I worked summers as a ranger with the Forest Service. From that experience, I knew that working the same ground year after year initiated a certain kind of intimacy with one's place. I knew that the same was true for many of the monks who worked this land, tending cattle or working in the alfalfa fields. I also knew that the real work for them, the work that sustained it all, was prayer.

As we rode out through the fields beyond the monastery in an old Datsun pickup, and as he told me about his work there, Father Joseph would occasionally turn his smile and glance my way. At eighty-two, he was still spry and full of energy. He was a short man. Even on the up-bounce from a truck bench that seemed a little lower than most, his gaze barely cleared the top of the steering wheel. His eyes were glacial lake blue. He wore green coveralls and a pith helmet, as did most of the monks in the old black and white farm work photos that hung on the guest house wall.

As we drove out toward the far edge of the alfalfa fields, he introduced me to an invading weed known as dyar's woad. It was a tall, spindly yellow-flowered weed, which had been encroaching on the Abbey's alfalfa fields and foothill pastures for some time. Left unabated, he told me, it choked out the good grasses that fed their cattle herd and the deer and elk that grazed those hillside meadows.

By the time we entered the mouth of a foothill draw, I learned that each of these weeds produced a thousand seeds, that they liked bare rocky ground, that some were annuals, some biennials, and some perennials, and that they needed to be cut before their seed pods turned brown. Father Joseph had consulted field extension agents and university professors, none of whom knew of an easier way to get rid of the stuff. In the foothill pastures ahead of us, he pointed out huge yellow patches where this invader was already well-established. It had also spread along either side of a pipeline, built by the monks shortly after their arrival back in 1947, which supplied the monastery with spring water. We parked the truck at the head of the draw and began to work our way up through tall grass and scrub oak. Swinging short-handled weed whackers as we went, forehand then backhand, forehand then backhand, we left behind fallen swaths of the dreaded woad. The air smelled like cut grass. Vultures circled overhead, much to Father Joseph's delight. "They get rid of the gophers," he hollered, as he whacked another clump of weeds to the ground. Gophers, he explained, dug up the ground, which created perfect growing conditions for the plant that had quickly become my nemesis. There was no end to the stuff, it seemed. But any futility I sensed in the job that lay before us hardly mattered on that afternoon in May.

What mattered was the joy of hard work under a blue sky with an elderly monk so clearly at home in those foothill meadows. What mattered were the wildflowers that lit up the hillside— purple phlox, lacy white yarrow, a wide swath of yellow daisies, red-orange flashes of Indian paintbrush. What mattered were the ruby-throated hummingbirds who flew straight up and dove straight down in the heat of their courtship passion. What mattered were the long and languid wing beats of the sandhill cranes who came drifting up the draw where they had been nesting, Father Joseph said, for the last ten years or so.

The weeds began to thin out as we worked our way up toward the rounded spine of a foothill ridge. "Yesterday was the forty-seventh anniversary of my arrival here," Father Joseph said as we topped out and looked out over the monastery grounds and the valley beyond. Farther west was the rocky crown of Mt. Ogden, still laced with streaks of snow. "I will always remember the day we got here . . . Here we were in July and that mountain top was covered with snow. I'd never seen anything like it."

We were now standing, he informed me, on the highest point of the Abbey's property. Below us a breeze rippled across the season's second crop of alfalfa, soon to be cut. "It's wonderful up here," he said. "Hard to put the feeling into words . . . God's greatness I guess."

I shared in that joy as we scoured the ridge. When work became a thank you for one's home, for one's place, for the sacrament of the present moment as it seemed to be for Father Joseph, and as it was for me as we contoured back down to the truck on that mountain morning, even weed-slashing could become a kind of celebration. In the context of prayer, and in the broad expanse of the Abbey's pastures, emptied of all, it seemed, but mountain and sky, even a moment of simple celebration had a deeper resonance.

"The Trappist life," Father Joseph told me, was "one of rustic simplicity." I could see that in the careful mending of his coveralls and in the jerry-rigged ignition button that he pushed to start that old relic of a Datsun. And I could hear that in the stories he told me, over seat springs creaking, as we rattled down that mountain road.

He still got up at around two o'clock each morning—a rhythm he said he had gotten used to back in the days when the monastery still had a herd of dairy cattle. He pointed to the barn that came back into view as we drove out the mouth of the draw and followed a ditch down toward the alfalfa. There had never been any heat where he did the milking. At two o'clock on a cold winter morning, everything in the milking shed was frozen. "Once all the cows were back in there," he said, "they gave off enough heat to warm the place up."

Over the eight years or so that he had managed the herd, he had delivered at least sixty, maybe as many as seventy, calves. "Not bad for a city kid," was his refrain, as he reminded me, and perhaps himself, of his urban roots back in Louisville, Kentucky.

I thought I heard a wistful tone in Father Joseph's words. Later on Brother David would confirm my hunch. As the Abbey's population had gotten older, many of the monastic work projects had been laid down—among them Father Bartholomew's bees, a substantial bread baking operation, and Father Joseph's dairy herd. The monks still had a sizable herd of beef cattle. They still produced a large alfalfa crop. They still fed and housed hundreds, if not thousands, of guests a year. And Father Joseph still missed that dairy herd.

Though he didn't milk cows any more, the pattern of rising early, even by monk standards, was still a part of his life. I had noticed, as we walked and worked together, that Father Joseph did not wear a watch. Still, he knew when it was time to head down the mountain. It wasn't long after we had parked the truck in the barn, that the monastery bells began to ring.

NEXT MORNING, I GOT UP WITH THE BELLS. VIGIL, THE FIRST GATH-ering for worship at the monastery each day, took place at 3:30am. I settled in, still a little groggy, next to an open window on the far side of the balcony overlooking the chapel and the monks. I heard a coyote in the distance. I heard the wind rising and falling with the cadence of the psalms. It was hard to tell where one left off and the other began. Maybe it was that way for some of the monks whose daily rhythms were so deeply intertwined with this place.

As always, the chapel was especially quiet and dark during vigil, except for the pool of light around the pulpit where Father Charles gave the morning's reading. He talked about preparing a room or a house in the heart and sweeping it clean, so that "the Holy Spirit might dwell in it." This, it seemed, was the inward equivalent of the kind of quiet and open space that the monastery offered visitors. In the face of a changing and unstable world, the monastery said in effect: here is something steady and constant.

Whether working on the ridgetop with Father Joseph, or in the Abbey chapel listening to the psalms, I was reminded of that space in the heart. And I was reminded of my need to tend to that space, in much the same way that the monks at the Abbey cared for their corner of this mountain valley.

Straight Ahead Till Morning

I KNEW FROM MY FRIENDSHIPS WITH THE MONKS AT THE ABBEY OF the Holy Trinity that there was much to be learned from good mentors. So I was especially pleased to find out about another elder with whom I had many interests in common—mountains and a contemplative life among them. I'd first learned of his career as priest, mountaineer, naturalist, and explorer in a Santa Fe motel room magazine. That we had a family connection— Father Anderson Bakewell was my father's first cousin—further encouraged me get to know the man I would later call the Padre.

The first time we talked on the phone, his hello was more growl than greeting, but his tone soon changed when he found out I was kin. He invited me up to a chapel near St. John's College in Santa Fe where he still offered mass most mornings. This little chapel, where he served as chaplain and priest for a community of mostly cloistered Carmelite nuns and a small but loyal congregation, was small and plain as Catholic churches go. It was brightly lit with simple wooden benches. On one side of the altar was a pulpit and a small tabernacle on the wall that held the sacraments. On the other side were the Carmelite nuns, who I heard without seeing as they sang on the far side of a screened partition.

Soon the Padre shuffled into the church. His steps and breathing were somewhat labored as he made his way to the altar. A young Hispanic boy brought him his vestment, which he flipped up into the air, his head finding the opening as it came down. He smoothed the wrinkles on his shoulders, brushed back a wisp of silver hair, and began the Mass. He had a tone of voice that he reserved for prayers and scripture readings. The way he elongated his E's and rolled his R's—Spirit became *"speeeerr-rit"*—made him sound more like an Anglican than a Catholic.

At home after Mass in a small casita a few streets south of the Santa Fe Plaza, the Padre seemed a lot less priestly. Though he was comfortable in his clerical garb, he told me that he generally preferred the company of naturalists, hunters, and mountaineers to that of his fellow priests. On his bedpost hung a nine-millimeter pistol, a boning knife, and a Mauser rifle. On a bedside chair was a typically eclectic assortment of books and journals— the *American Alpine Journal*, the Bible, the *Social Register*, and *National Geographic*. The NRA sticker on the back bumper of the old mustang that he drove to church and back came as no surprise. Elk and moose heads hung on his walls. The hide of a black bear taken in the Alaskan backcountry and a mountain lion taken with a bow on the Jicarilla Apache Reservation covered his floor. He had a taste for game of every kind—the wilder the meat, the better. And he liked his Yukon Jack.

Eagerly anticipating our breakfast conversation, I had fired up the skillet, scrambled some eggs, and fried up some bear sausage, compliments of my in-laws up in Mancos, Colorado. In the subdued light of his den-like casita, the Padre shuffled over to his chair and settled his hulk in at the head of the table. It occurred to me that he had a few characteristics in common with the bear whose hide now lay on his floor. In an adobe alcove above the breakfast table, I noticed another minature bear carved out of quartz next to a small wooden cross. Images that might have seemed a little incongruent placed side by side in someone else's life, made perfect sense here.

I set two plates of breakfast on the table. The Padre offered a blessing and we settled into a conversation about the family tree. He told me about my grandfather, his uncle, who had been quite a sportsman in a mid-western bird-hunting kind of a way. "It's in the genes," said the Padre.

I asked the Padre about his call to ministry, how it had come about, what had led him to the Jesuits. His response was simple: "You do what you're asked to do." This was one of those times— many more would follow—when he made it clear, speaking in a deliberate and emphatic way, that there was nothing else to be said on the matter. If there was a little ambiguity as to who had asked him to become a priest, a prayer he taught me later—"Tell me what you want me to do, God, and give me the guts to do it"—would clear that up.

Later, I told the Padre I had been drawn to the Quaker community and the contemplative way of worship I found there. Given the absence of Friends on the family tree, this was something of a genealogical mutation. He reminded me of my Catholic roots by way of my grandfather (his uncle). I had the feeling that he had his hopes for me. "It's in the genes," he would say again, leaving me to decide what "it" was and thinking, I imagined, that an interest in the contemplative tradition would eventually bring me home to the fold.

Unlike me, the Padre had a strong connection to his religious roots. His grandfather once took communion from Father Pierre-Jean De Smet, the legendary trailblazer, missionary and Jesuit priest who set out for the Rocky Mountains in 1840. Received well by the Flathead and Pend d'Oreilles tribes, and subsequently almost every Indian nation with whom he had contact, De Smet would eventually serve them as an advocate and as a peacemaker. For a Catholic kid like Andy Bakewell growing up in St. Louis back in the 1920s, Father de Smet would have been almost as celebrated as Lewis and Clark. Although the Padre never told me directly, he inferred that growing up under the influence of all that Jesuit lore had planted the seed for decisions he would make later on.

Breakfast set aside, the Padre called for a shot of Yukon Jack. Ten o'clock in the morning might have seemed a little early to some. Then again, early in the morning was a relative term. For the Padre, the day began at around three AM with a period of Jesuit devotions—a disciplined regimen of prayers and meditations. Looking around the Padre's casita, I saw, amidst all the hides and heads, a mix of religious objects he had collected during his travels. The small cross in that adobe alcove, I would learn, had come from a Christian community in India. A statue of Mary on the altar had come from Mexico. An icon of Mary that he had placed on an altar along the far wall was the work of a local friend named Jack Good—Icon Jack as the Padre liked to call him.

Only Yukon Jack made an appearance at breakfast that first day. Having toasted one another, and with the afterglow of a little Yukon heat in the belly, we got to talking about mountains. I knew that he had several first ascents to his credit in North and South America. I knew that he had traveled to the south side of Everest to scout out an approach several years before Hillary and Norgay made the summit. How was it, I wondered, that a kid from the flatlands of Missouri had come to be such an accomplished mountaineer?

The Padre told me about early summers spent at his grandfather's lodge in Estes Park, Colorado, and how he had taken to the high country at first as a way of recovering his strength after teenage bouts with an inner ear affliction called mastoiditis. Along the way he had picked up some mountaineering skills, culminating in a climb up the east face of Long's Peak in 1933. That, he said, was right about the time that he'd started working with Marlin Perkins and the St Louis Zoological Society. "Take a look in that box over there in the corner," he said. Which one? His casita was busting at the seams with cardboard boxes of books and papers on everything from theology to mountaineering. After digging through several boxes full of Bakewell memorabilia, I found the photo he was after. He was pictured with Marlin, who looked a good deal younger than the Marlin I remembered from the *Wild Kingdom* television show I watched when I was a kid.

Soon he was telling me about a snake-collecting trip with Marlin into the Ozark Mountains . . . how they had once ducked into a cave during a storm and passed the time playing jacks with rattlesnake vertebrae. Had it not been for the pain and discomfort that periodically plagued his eighty-two year old body, a body, I would learn, that was riddled with arthritis as well as cancer, he would have had many more stories to tell that morning.

"Hold on," he said as he grimaced in pain. "It'll pass." I was relieved when he seemed to relax a few moments later. Though the pain, whatever the source, seemed to have passed, he still looked tired and I didn't want to wear him down. The Padre took care of that. "Pedro," he said. "I think we'd better call it a day."

THE PADRE TIRED EASILY. CANCER—THE BIG C AS HE CALLED IT— had taken several of his brothers. His own prostate cancer was well advanced, according to the doctor I would speak with on the phone later that year, having heard that the Padre had checked himself into the hospital for a few days. But he wasn't one to buckle under to a little pain. Nor was he one to close his door to the world. He had no intention of retiring from his vocation, part of which was the gift of hospitality that he offered whenever he was physically able.

Anytime we drove down from our Salt Lake City home to visit with my wife's family in southwestern Colorado, I would try and break away for a few days to visit the Padre. A desire to hear and record his stories, a growing interest in matters of the Spirit, and a strong wish to make the most of whatever time our growing friendship had left, would lead me from that little chapel at St. Johns to the door of his casita, into his kitchen, and back to those breakfast table conversations. This was the routine we would later call homilies and grits.

Always generous with his life, he gave me plenty of homework—folders and scrapbooks full of photos, old newspaper clips, letters. How he was able to find anything in that cardboard box filing system of his was beyond me. No doubt he had a lot of help from Lisa, a friend and caretaker who made sure he got fed and medicated and kept up with his correspondence. Both the Padre and I knew that our time was limited. And we had a lot of ground to cover in his life alone. So I took my homework seriously and brought plenty of questions to the breakfast table each morning.

The mountain trails the Padre recalled took us back to a jungle in northern India where he had taken one of his first assignments—that of assistant priest at a remote Jesuit outpost. In the tradition of Father De Smet, he was devoted to serving those on the margins, packing his Mass kit and a satchel and walking from village to village, often alone and sometimes at night, for months at a time. I'd never really seen the need for religious proselytizing. Then again, Quakers were so low-profile that many folks associated us with oatmeal and oil changes.

But the Padre's style differed from that of the stereotypical missionary who was all mouth and no ear. As St. Ignatius, founder of the Jesuit Order, once put it: "we do not preach . . . we speak familiarly of spiritual things with a few, as one does after dinner, with those who invite us." This was the Padre's way. It was a way that had taken him through terrain inhabited by panthers, tigers, and sloth bears, not to mention scorpions, kraits, cobras and other crawling critters. His willingness to travel alone under the circumstances impressed many of the villagers in northern India to whom he brought Mass.

So too would an incident at a place called Bhaludungri. Bhaludungri, which means *Bear Hill*, was an isolated rock outcrop covered with jungle scrub where problem bears took refuge after reeking havoc in nearby villages. The Padre had joined in on the hunt for a sloth bear that had attacked a young boy. Of all the wild inhabitants of the region, sloth bears were feared the most, due in apart to their unpredictability and in part to their tendency, according to local lore, to rip off the scalps of any unfortunate humans who got in their way. That this bear had already attacked, and had subsequently been wounded, made this hunt up Bear Hill all the more treacherous.

One night, I came across a photograph of a sloth bear's skull. I didn't realize, until I heard his story the next morning, that the teeth in that skull had once been embedded in the Padre's leg. "Following up a wounded bear can lead to trouble, especially in thick cover," he said over a lingering cup of coffee. "But we had no choice. We wanted to find the bear before it found a woman gathering firewood or a child herding cattle." He paused. Whether intended or not, it added to the anticipation of the bear encounter he was about to describe.

"Some say that a charging sloth bear will stop short and rise on its hind feet before it attacks," he told me, "but this one hadn't read that script." He heard the roar of the bear before he actually saw it——only ten paces away and coming on fast. The Padre got off a shot. But, he said, "the bear, came in low, fastened his teeth on my left thigh, put the claws of his paw in the calf of the same leg, and threw his weight into the tackle."

During the time that I knew the Padre, I would hear different versions of what happened next. It may have been that the first bullet finally took effect. It may have been that another man rushed in to distract the bear. In the chaos that followed their first encounter, the bear paused and backed off long enough for the Padre to get off another shot . . . this one finishing the job that the first had only begun. Father Julius Kujur, with whom the Padre had been working at their jungle outpost, turned up in time to translate the reaction of the locals who had gathered at the scene: "They don't understand the Padre," Kujur told his wounded comrade. "The blood is running down his leg and he is laughing."

HUNTING WASN'T THE ENDGAME FOR THE PADRE, ANY MORE THAN mountaineering had been. They were both part of a much bigger exploration—one that began now with his morning devotions and radiated from there. Memories alone covered plenty of territory, but prayer took him even further. Near that altar, on which he had placed those icons of Mary, those crosses, and those candles often lit, was a big photo of the earth as seen from the moon, signed by one of the astronauts who had been there looking back. He noticed me looking at the photo and recited his favorite haiku:

Behold the hunter returns.
In his game bag he carries
the moon and the stars.

The Padre's sense of place took in those far fields of the stars.
Back in the early 1940s, he had written an article for the *American Alpine Journal* speculating on possible routes up the mountains of the moon. In a universe where God was limitless, so too was the potential for exploration. Space led him into that meditation.

So did his travels above timberline. The Padre seemed to understand those momentary openings in high places that I had always struggled to name. Part of the mountain experience, he suggested, had to do with the perception of beauty, which was often a prelude to prayer. Quoting from a theological treatise known as the *circumincessio amoris*, he gave me words that I would write in my journal later that night. "Beauty born of God. Goes out from God. Is caught like a mirror by the human mind. Returned by the human heart in love and Thanksgiving." Put that way, the perception and appreciation of beauty was a necessary link in the circular relationship between that which was human and that which was holy. To be fully present on the mountain was to enter into that motion of love.

OVER THE COURSE OF OUR VISITS, THE PADRE DUG THROUGH ALL HIS cardboard boxes and scrapbooks and before long I had a folder full of photos that followed his lifeline from the Yukon to Nepal to a mountain in the back country of the High Sierras where he held Mass, over the North and South Poles in an airplane (the first such flight), and eventually up north to mountains and tundra of Alaska. In the science section of *Life Magazine* (November 20, 1939), between a smiling housewife holding up a shiny new Toastmaster and Aunt Jemima holding a platter of pancakes, were aerial photos of Yukon rivers and glaciers, tents nearly buried at ten thousand feet on Mt. Wood. And there was a portrait of the Wood expedition members, including the Padre, arms folded, leaning back against a rock, smiling in a splash of sun (which had been a rarity on that particular expedition).

In 1985, forty-six years later, a newspaper photo from the Whitehorse Star pictured a Padre long retired from those high peaks. He had come back to the St. Elias Range, this time as a guest of honor at a ceremony honoring the accomplishments of pioneer mountaineers whose first ascents up the mountains in what had since become Kluane National Park were legendary. In the dedication he offered to his fellow mountaineers, the Padre spoke of Elijah, "mountain pioneer" of the Old Testament, for whom the St. Elias Mountains had been named. Like Elijah, who listened for God in the midst of wind, earthquake, and fire before hearing the still small voice in a gentle breeze, the Padre reminded those present that Jesus had often prayed on a mountain. "Lord Jesus Christ," he prayed, "son of the living God. Look kindly on us gathered here today: men who love your mountains."

For the Padre, a love of mountains and a love of God seemed to animate one another. Of all his adventures, none were any more inspirational than his trek to a Buddhist monastery or lamasery a few miles south of Mt. Everest, which was known locally, he reminded me, as Chomolunga—"Goddess Mother of the World." A photo taken in 1950, a year before his ordination in India, showed the soon-to-be-Padre looking downright natty in trekking shoes, knee socks, khaki shorts, and a button-down wool jacket. He was posing near that monastery, in front of an ice scoured slope of stone, with Bill Tillman, the great English mountaineer and explorer, Betsy Cowles, one of

America's foremost female climbers holding a camera of her own, Oscar Houston, a New York lawyer and member of the American Alpine Club who had initiated this expedition to the south side of Everest, and his son Dr. Charles Houston who had climbed with Tillman on a previous expedition to Nanda Devi. Although a handful of Westerners had been through that part of Nepal, none of them, in recent history anyway, had approached this monastery on the southern flanks of Everest.

It was as if the Padre had walked into *Lost Horizon*, the classic novel about a handful of westerners who survive a plane crash in the Himalayas and discover a seemingly timeless culture there. The tale from the book he always loved to tell me had to do with one of the first encounters between a monk and one of the Westerners, who asked: "What do you do here?"

"We pray and seek wisdom," said the monk

"But that's not really doing anything," said the Westerner.

"In that case," said the monk, "we do nothing."

When the Padre and his fellow trekkers finally arrived at Tengboche Gompa, after many miles, two weeks, and over seventy thousand feet of up-then-down-then-up-again elevation gain, the lamas (or monks) who had apparently heard from nearby villagers that these adventurers were on their way, turned out to greet them and offer shelter. And a welcome shelter it was. After a day of slogging up the mountain through a heavy wet snow, a roaring fire in a large room above a stable, hot tea made and delivered by the lamas (who would continue to honor their guests with gifts and hospitality over the course of their stay), a good meal, and a few hot toddies, made for plenty of good cheer.

Night winds winnowed the sky of clouds. Next morning, the day broke clear and shutters were opened to reveal the monastery ground covered with a fresh snow. Beyond the last of the buildings, beyond the yaks pastured in an otherwise entirely white foreground, were the great shining ridges of the Himala-yas—-Kantega (22,340 ft.) and Damserki (21,130 ft)—towering over the monastery and notched into the deepest and bluest sky the Padre had ever seen. He described the scene further to the north at the head of the valley: "behind a steep ridge of rock and ice around 25,000 feet high, loomed a familiar, tilted pyra-midal shape; the summit of our planet."

Long before daylight, he set out for a steep and rocky ridge with Pa Nurbu, one of the expedition Sherpas. As the sun rose he saw above him a small shrine, or *chorten*, lit up and haloed in a brilliant white light. Later on during that climb, he discovered that hoar frost gathered on the branches which held the prayer flags at the top of the chorten, caught and refracted the light in that way. Pressing on, they would reach an altitude of 17,000 feet, from which only the high tip of Everest was visible, some eight miles to the north, as were the great plumes of snow that the wind carried up from its summit. That cloud banner was the "prayer flag" that the Padre would bring home from the highest mountain on the planet, seen only from a distance, but never forgotten.

THE ELUSIVE SUMMIT—"THE LITTLE PLOT FOR WHICH WE WAX SO fierce"—is an apt symbol for seekers and mountaineers who have known those moments and places where the holy feels especially close at hand. A photo taken in 1966 shows the Padre holding Mass while on retreat in the High Sierra. In his retreat notes, he recalled the words of a fellow mountaineering partner in the Yukon: "Roger Drury once said that if it is the function of an angel to stand and give glory to God; then *in that sense*, every tree is an angel." The Padre wasn't one to suggest that trees should never be logged or put to use any more than he would have denied a hunter his food. But he knew that a tree, or any other aspect of creation for that matter, was an invitation into awe and wonder, maybe even prayer.

On a snowy slope above Tyndall Creek in the High Sierra, where he had laid out the sacraments on a flat-topped boulder, he observed the light of the rising sun streaming through the lodgepole pines. In the Padre's theology, the existence of the created universe, in and of itself, gave glory to God. As he explained it to me, this was referred to as material glory which, he pointed out, was also described in the Hindu Upanishads: "The Universe is the glory of God and all that lives and moves therein." As the Padre explained it, glory was what Teillard de Chardin described as the "shining through" of the Transcendent One.

While the Padre saw his vocation as taking the Word out into the world, he also knew that the world was, in a sense, bringing the Word to us as well. But you had to get out there to know that. In 1967, an opportunity to do so came his way. The photo shows him standing in front of The Pole Cat, a Boeing 707, that would carry him, along with forty other scientists, over both poles and around the globe in what was then record breaking time: sixty-two hours and twenty seven minutes.

On this first flight over both poles, the Padre rode in the belly of the plane operating NASA equipment that measured the earth's reflective capacity. But it was his priestly work—offering prayers before and after the journey, as well as the Mass he gave in flight—which meant the most to him. "We asked you to bless this aircraft . . . to shield us as we encircled the planet . . . in our search for knowledge of the mysteries of your creation," he said in a ceremony held upon landing in Honolulu. "You have done all that we asked and we are sincerely and humbly grateful."

In one of the newspaper articles given me by the Padre, veteran newscaster, global traveler, and mountain enthusiast Lowell

Thomas referred to the Pole Cat's flight around the world and over the poles as "the last great adventure." That phrase gave me pause. The Padre, had come of age with some the twentieth century's most renowned explorers and mountaineers—people like Sir Edmund Hillary and George Mallory were his contemporaries. At that time, many of the biggest peaks in North and South America had yet to be climbed. Territories like the Yukon were still being mapped. By the time I caught up with the Padre in the 1990s, expeditions to Everest were increasingly commercialized and outdoor "adventure" of all sorts had become an industry. By the time we met, you could locate yourself on the map by way of a satellite signal and you could call your loved ones on the telephone from the top of Mt. Everest.

As I pondered all of this, I was reminded of a comment mountaineer Reinhold Messner once made. The wildest edge of exploration in our time, at least on this planet, he suggested, was an inward one—the terrain of the heart, a geography known best, he said, by monks and others who had embarked on the great interior adventure.

Maybe so. Part of what had attracted me to the Padre was the way his life had embodied the adventure "out there" with the inward work of prayer. Just as religion without some sense of adventure left me cold, so too did adventure without the kind of inward outlook that encouraged an appreciation of the great wonder and mystery of it all. "All that any one talks about any more is their gear," said the Padre during one of our last visits. In his cut-to-the-chase kind of way, he gathered his thoughts in a few simple words: "Without an interior life, you might as well hang up your skates."

As it turned out, we would have several more visits after that first week together. I remember one of the last times we saw the Padre, he was tethered up to an oxygen tank which rankled his independent spirit. On that same visit, he let out a spirited celebratory whoop when we told him that Grace was pregnant.

"Whoever this little soul is, they'll be putting in some mountain time," I said.

"It's in the genes," he said, as he offered our child-to-be his blessing.

In October of 1999, just a few months short of the millennial summit that he had hoped to reach, I received word of his death. Grace and I drove out to St. Louis for the memorial service. Under turning leaves and a clear blue October sky, I helped carry his casket to a gravesite only a few hundred feet up the hill from the ground where my grandfather and my father's twin brother had been buried.

On the window sill above my desk is the silver hip flask he gave me. It has a few dents, a little solder here and there. I know it held a lot of Yukon Jack. I like to think that shots were poured on Mt. Wood up there in the Yukon, on the way in to Everest, or in his Alaskan parish after a rescue mission at seventy below.

Not long ago, I turned the page in an old journal and one of the last clippings that he had given me fell onto my desk: "Action presupposes contemplation: it springs from the latter and is nourished by it. Love cannot be given to one's brothers and sisters unless it has first been drawn from the genuine source . . . ."

I thought back on that short walk up the Padre's last hill, the beginning of what he understood as the grand ascent to that source. "Death is nothing to worry about," he once said in a homily. "Peter Pan had it right: it's out the window, second turn to the right, and straight ahead till morning."

Part Two: Explorations

Excelsior: A Prelude

*"When the inner and the outer are one, and the above is
like the below . . . then you will enter the kingdom."*

—*Gospel According to St. Thomas*

THOUGH I HAD TRIED TO LISTEN, AS FAR AS I KNEW, I HAD NEVER
heard God's words directly. What I had heard were words,
inwardly or spoken by someone else, which seemed deeply
real and true; words that were in alignment with the spirit of
wisdom and compassion as Jesus had embodied it; words, like
C.S. Lewis' signposts, that seemed to nudge me toward wholeness and therefore, as I understood it, toward God.

In Indiana, we lived in a house full of words like this. On
the day that Grace and I had moved into George and Ellen
Klemperer's old house on Chanticleer Farm, I noticed, on the
kitchen bulletin board, these typewritten verses from the German
poet Rilke:

My eyes already touch the sunny hill,
Going far ahead of the road I have begun.
So if we are grasped by what we cannot grasp;
it has its inner light, even from a distance—

And changes us, even if we do not reach it,
Into something else, which, hardly sensing it, we already are:
A gesture waves us on, answering our own wave . . .
but what we feel is the wind in our faces.

It wasn't long before I made the connection between Rilke's poem and the western horizon as seen out the kitchen window. Beyond the lawn and whitewashed fence, beyond the maple that went brilliant red from the top down each October, and beyond the rolling field which was planted some years in corn, and some years in winter wheat, there was a hill, several hundred feet high, that Grace and I came to know as the mound. It looked to me like a drumlin, one of those egg-shaped hills left behind by the moving ice of a glacier. And that seemed to fit in with the little bit of local geology I knew, namely that the farm would have been close to the edge of the icy glacial moraines which had come down from the north and which had eventually receded in that direction.

We'd been told that lots of Indian artifacts had been found out around the mound. That too made sense, since it would have been a preferred vantage point in this neck of the woods.

Always it was the reference point on our circuitous walks along the fenclines that defined the edge of the farm or on longer forays down to the Whitewater River farther to the west. Often we saw wild turkeys out that way. One spring, we walked the slopes of the mound gathering chanterelle mushrooms. When the sun hit top of the mound in the morning I was reminded of Ellen and the Rilke verses she had posted on the bulletin board. This, I imagined, was her "sunny hill."

We were the first to live in Ellen's house after her death, and her presence lingered. Shortly after we moved in, a lamp kept turning on by itself one night. Those who had known Ellen

acknowledged her depth of spirit and I wondered, each time the
light went on, if she was offering her greeting from the other
side. The next day, I did find a short in the lamp cord. But in
a way that was irrelevant. Light or no light, Ellen had already
gotten my attention.

As the weeks passed, I would learn that Ellen had been a
respected spiritual presence and mentor in the Richmond
Quaker community, "a weighty Friend" in Quaker parlance.
While working in an archive back east, a new seminary friend
of mine remembered reading some of Ellen's letters to Howard
Thurman, the great African-American theologian and mystic
who had been her mentor and spiritual guide and whose works
she had helped to publish and promote. Her descendants, our
neighbors on the farm, also told us stories about Ellen and welcomed us to the house on her behalf: "She would be so happy
to have you here."

It did seem to be a good fit. I knew, based on her library alone,
that Ellen's spiritual interests were akin to our own. I knew
also from reading the notes she left in the margins of her many
books—heavily weighted toward contemplatives, poets, depth
psychologists, and other explorers of the interior—that she
would have had much to teach us. I knew of her struggles with
George's early death from a farm accident, not to mention her
own bout with cancer. I could surmise from her readings, that she
had struggled at times with a sense of emptiness, if not despair.

But I imagined, too, that her trials led her further down the road
of the Spirit Rilke had written about in those verses on the bulletin board. Many a time during those seminary years we spent out
at the farm, I would notice that poem and find in it some reassurance in knowing that others had traveled a road less easily named
or explained perhaps, but as real as the sun on the mound or the
wind that met us as we walked across the field toward it.

Along the eastern edge of the mound, passing the fenced-in graves where Ellen and George had been buried, I would also think of Rilke's poem, imagining as I did that those words, Ellen's seeking, and the sun that found the top of the mound each morning, had all been conjoined for her somehow on this heartland farm. For a while, Ellen's home was for us a dwelling place and a refuge. But as another year at seminary came to an end each spring, right about the time the first wave of fireflies would appear, Ellen's hill, and the words she left on her bulletin board, were a gesture waving us on, as we drove back out onto Highway 27, and turned west toward the Rockies.

Last Light Falling

AFTER PITCHING THE TENT, COOKING DINNER, AND SETTLING IN ON the edge of the alpine meadow just beyond the trees from my old base camp here in the High Uintas, I light a cigar and blow a puff of smoke out toward the red light riding the crest of a snow-coned peak called Mt. Emmons. On the far side of this mountain, driving east on Highway 40 at the beginning of every summer season I worked here as a ranger for the Forest Service, I could tell, judging from the snowpack on the south side of Mt. Emmons, how long it would be before we would get up through the middle elevations and into the high country where I now stand. That kind of familiarity reassured me then, as does this ritual smoke on the edge of my favorite alpine meadow now, that even a wanderer can know the steadying welcome of home ground.

For much of my life, a strong sense of home has eluded me. It may be in the genes, as the Padre used to say. Where once both sides of my family were well-rooted, one in Missouri, the other in Mississippi, more recent generations have hit the road, leaving behind a long list of forwarding addresses. Early signs of wanderlust turned up in the family story by way of Stephen Allen Bemis, my great-great grandfather who rode a steamer to

Nicaragua, worked in the gold fields of the Sierra, went home to Illinois for a short spell, and then drove a herd of cattle across the Great Plains. "The spirit of roving was strong within me," he wrote. "I was not able to resist it."

I came down on his side of the family tree. Growing up in a suburban Long Island home, part of our family lore had to do with the fact that we weren't really locals. At least we weren't locals like most of the families we knew, who had been on the north shore of Long Island for generations. My parents were both from Pennsylvania. Their parents were from the south and the midwest. So we were a few moves and a generation or two distant from any kind of meaningful roots. As it turned out, my parents would relocate to Florida. My sister and I would go west, to Washington and Colorado, respectively. We were a clan on the move. Maybe as great grandfather Bemis said, it had to do with that roving spirit. I, for one, had not been "able to resist it."

So home, for me, is a dream line that runs through seven states, three cities, and eleven small towns. It runs through forty-eight years, less than half of them east of the Mississippi River, more than half of them out west. At the center of my story is an ongoing query. And that query—"Where you from?"—easily segues into others like "Who are you?" and "What do you believe?"

Even though I only worked here for five backcountry seasons, and even though I spent most of the year a hundred miles or so to the west in Salt Lake City writing and teaching, this corner of the High Uinta Wilderness in northern Utah became a temporary form of home ground. Each year, I knew I would find the gang of four bull moose who ran together around Kidney Lakes or the nest of ptarmigan up in Painter Basin or a particularly lovely clump of purple alpine flowers (moss campion) near the top of Trailrider Pass.

In this part of Utah, where locals horse-pack into the same

high country camp year after year, I came to recognize many of the other backcountry regulars, as they had come to recognize me: "Oh yeah . . . you were coming over from Davis Lakes when I saw you last year." We were a community, albeit seasonal and migratory, moving up the Uinta River with the thaw in the early summer, and coming down with the snowline in the fall.

Even now, almost four years since I worked my last season here, I can come here to remember what it feels like to belong to a place. Samuels Creek runs down the middle of this high mountain meadow (11,000 feet). I follow its course, walking through low clumps of willow and across marshy tussocks that would swallow my steps during a normal year. Even though it is drier this season, great swaths of a flower known as elephant's head, a little more wilted than usual, still tint the meadow pink. As always, I find plenty of elk sign. Last night, I savored the high bleating sounds of the cows and calves calling to one another out here.

On the far side of the meadow, in among some widely-spaced spruce, I can see the remains of the old cabin-like structure, on which I would hang an old wall tent when I worked here as a ranger. Other than the porcupine that sometimes came by late at night to gnaw on the plywood floor beneath me (loudly and with great gusto), this was a mighty comfortable backcountry camp given the minimalist backpacking approach I was used to. With a little horse support, I would pack in a sheepherder's stove for heat, a big coffeepot, a few canned delicacies like sliced pineapples, and a railroad lantern for reading and writing on a desk top that dropped down from an old wooden cabinet. Every ranger on the district had a similar backcountry setup. Such "luxury" was justified in part by the weather (the High Uintas caught a lot of big storm moisture coming out of the south and southwest), by the mosquitoes for which the range was notorious, and by tradition, which still held sway on the Roosevelt District of the Ashley National Forest, where horseshoes tracked the trails more than hiking boots.

On my way into the trail head this time, I stopped by the old guard station which, for five years, had been the "halfway house" between working the backcountry and heading into the towns of the Uinta Basin, where we went to do our paper work at the end of every ten-day stint on the mountain and where we would stock up on groceries in preparation for our next "tour" (as in tour of duty). I had halfway expected to see a familiar Forest Service face or two. I thought I might find Shorty or Mark or one of the other Forest Service horses out in the corral behind the guard station. But the corrals were quiet. And the guard station, a vintage CCC cabin, was empty. Through the window, I could see that the old map, covering the contours of my summer range, still hung on the wall behind the kitchen stove.

A mile or so up the road at the trail head, I shouldered my pack. Just above the U-Bar Guest Ranch, I came to a familiar gate in an old wooden fence, intended to keep restless or runaway stock from heading down canyon. I'd always thought the gate was a fine piece of mountain woodcraft—the top of which had been worn smooth by all the hands that had opened and closed it. I especially liked the old horseshoe at the end of a rusted chain that I slid around the post as I closed the gate behind me. The act of opening and closing the gate had always struck me as a momentary acknowledgment of the long walk ahead or, on the way out, the nearness of trail's end.

This time I had savored the familiarity of the Uinta River trail, ambling up to Rock Creek where I saw the ever-present water ousel wheeling and swerving and dipping down into the spray that kicks up from the cascades underneath the bridge; passing the opening along the edge of the Uinta River gorge where violet green swallows, snapping up invisible insects, flew pirouettes around one another; passing dozens of waterbars (little check dams made of stone or wood) which I had put in to keep the trail from eroding on rocky hillsides; passing the Dugway, a loose shaley stretch of trail, which I had shoveled out once or twice every summer; passing the turn near the creek, where I'd once hauled water in a pack burro's leaky panniers to put out an abandoned campfire that was spreading quickly through the pine-needled duff; and walking through the big fir and spruce, blue sky now filling in the spaces between them, telling me I would soon be in this alpine meadow where I now stand.

From this meadow looking east toward Fox-Queant Pass and west toward Painter Basin and King's Peak (the highest peak in Utah), I can see that I am at the bottom of a U-shaped glacial cradle. At my feet, I see striations etched into flat slabs of bedrock, evidence of long gone ice in motion. Where the ice left off, the river has continued, grinding out the gorge now hidden from my sight by the fir and spruce down canyon.

There are still patches of snow on Mt. Emmons, the top of which I can see about ten miles to the south and west of the meadow as the crow flies. Here the light is pure and clear and there is more of it—around twenty percent more light at this elevation than at sea level. I am almost a mile closer to the sun at eleven thousand feet than in downtown Roosevelt where the district office is. Here, there is also more topography to catch the light and hold it than there is in the Basin twenty miles or so to the south of the guard station.

The skies back down in the basin look a little washed out now, if not over-exposed, compared to a deeper blue edging into violet overhead. If one could keep on climbing above the highest peak and into the stratosphere, artist John Van Dyke once said, one would see the sky turn ever darker shades of blue, then violet, then indigo, and on into the darkness of space.

As a seeker, I went to seminary, hoping to learn more about the inward geography of prayer and the Quaker tradition. As a wanderer, I have come back to the High Uintas, eager to know again the steadying welcome of home ground.

Knowing this place in a seasonal way is a longstanding tradition hereabouts. In that sense, I feel some kinship with the hunter who centuries ago came up here to stalk bighorn sheep. Working on an archaeological survey as a ranger, I once wandered up on a high bluff above a nearby lake and found a small pile of brown chert, flakes that had fallen to the ground while the hunter chipped away at a spear point. At that time, it was one of the highest archaeological sites in the state of Utah. The excitement I felt in finding it was not unlike like that moment after a cutthroat trout rises to your fly, and your rod bends down, and you savor the charge that runs through the line and into your hands. But the charge I felt from these flakes of stone left behind by the hunter many centuries ago, ran through time instead of water. And it came from another human being.

Back in his day, family life was limited to the lower elevations, say around seven or eight thousand feet, down in the Ponderosa pine forest. The high country was mostly the hunter's terrain. On the way in, he too might have felt restless coming through the middle elevations where the lodgepole pines creak and grown in the slightest wind and where the light falls only in broken flickers. As one archaeologist put it, this was the "dead zone" for Fremont hunters who walked the terrain a thousand years ago. In the lodgepoles, there would have been few large mammals to hunt, few edible plants to gather. Maybe the hunter was eagerly anticipating a bigger sky. Maybe he too would have been glad to break out of the trees and into this meadow.

But the hunter's destination would have been higher still.

If you were to head up toward the high ridges surrounding my camp, you would come first to the edge of the treeline. There you would find fir and spruce whose growth has been stunted by high winds and otherwise marginal growing conditions. This is known as the krummmholz zone. (*Krummholz* is a German word that means *elfin timber*). Here the trees fan out horizontally, growing away from the prevailing winds. The result is a shrub-like forest that would have offered the hunter good cover and decent shelter—a good base, in other words, for stalking the bighorn sheep that would occasionally come down from higher ground.

The krummholz zone is an edge on the way to an even higher edge, the one where the mountain leaves off and the sky beings. Today, there are still patches of bright white snow on those high ridges. John Van Dyke described the color of mountain snow "as the highest and last degree of whiteness. Nothing," he said, "went beyond or could exceed it." Similarly, nothing goes "beyond or can exceed" the high edge of a mountain watershed. Many wisdom traditions consider this edge to be the meeting place of the human and the holy. "When you get to the top of the mountain," says the Zen master, "keep on climbing."

I am not a hunter. But I am a wanderer and a seeker. And so I am drawn to this edge. Today I am seeking out the hunter's perch—one of them anyway—near the treeline. I am walking a ridge several miles from camp and almost a thousand feet higher in elevation, where there are scattered clumps of krummholz. And I am picturing the big slab of bedrock near one such clump where I found the flakes of chert that he left behind. It has been almost five years. I am hoping that his work has not been carted off and placed in a cigar box collection somewhere. I want to know his place again.

As is often the case around here, dark storm clouds are rising overhead. In the High Uintas, wandering up around the treeline late in the afternoon can be a crapshoot. So I have limited time. I walk faster.

Eyes scanning the ground, I am about to lose hope when I walk between two twisted spruce shrubs and out into a small clearing. There, in a little basin of bedrock, I see a small pile of chert, and I bend down to feel again these smooth flakes of stone the hunter left behind. The wind is picking up now. So I hunker down in this krummholz clearing, finding some of the shelter that the hunter might have known. I close my eyes, holding a piece of his chert, imagining the hunter offering a prayer here.

But it is hard for me to sit still. The wind has just picked up again. I open my eyes to clouds that look darker. So I pull on an extra layer, replace the stone, and bow to the hunter's ground before I drop down off the ridge. I scan the forest below me for a fast route back to camp. In the distance I can see the far edge of the meadow and it occurs to me that "edge" is a relative term. From a lowland perspective, my camp is an edge, from my camp the krummholz, and from the krummholz, the ridge tops above me. None of these edge lands offer more than a temporary residence at best.

Maybe it is the same with prayer. It too is a temporary dwelling place. At least that's the way I experience it. In prayer, or in the silence of Quaker meeting, crossing the inward edge that leads into deeper realms of stillness is like breaking out of the trees and walking into an alpine meadow. Deeper yet, it is like leaving the trees behind for the higher elevations. And at some point, the inward experience feels like a night walk on an alpine ridge. One is still grounded, but in the shadowed lands up ahead, or in the star light reflected in a lake below, it isn't always easy to tell where the mountain leaves off and the sky begins.

The weather turns cold and rainy. I stay close to camp, wondering how the hunter would have fared under the cover of a krummholz canopy. The clouds have hunkered down on the ridges. I can no longer see Mount Emmons. The storm comes through in waves, allowing only for an occasional short walk through the meadow. For the better part of day, I am tent-bound.

This is nothing new in the High Uintas. My first season, the rains were steady all summer. I can recall only a few days when it didn't rain. Back then, a coffee pot on the sheepherder's stove and the sound of rain on the canvas roof of the wall tent were fine comfort. This time around, I set up a little camp chair in a much smaller tent, wrap myself in a sleeping bag, and take out some reading material that I have packed in, anticipating a day or two like this. A few words, whether read or written, are a good antidote for tent fever—that affliction in which one's shelter feels smaller and smaller as the rainy hours pass.

So for a while I read Douglas Steere, a Quaker writer whose explorations of the Spirit have offered me much guidance, and whose words, I'm guessing, may continue to speak, as I close my eyes and settle into an hour or so of quiet listening. What I hear in this time of prayer, and what I carry with me for the rest of the day, is: stilling the mind and body as one enters into prayer is good, but these are "vestibule exercises." The best way to cross the threshold into prayer, Steere says, is to enter into an awareness of being "immersed in a love that is utterly without qualification." This is God's love, he says. It is the equivalent of home ground in the heart's inmost center.

How often have I really known that kind of home ground? It is one thing to feel loved by another human being. That I have known in family, in friendship, in marriage. My daughter's hand reaching out for mine only minutes after she was born, felt like a love transcending conscious human awareness or intention.

But Steere is describing a level of spiritual intimacy that I'm not sure I have known. If I have known it, I have never been able to say unequivocally that it was the "Big G" I was experiencing.

So I puzzle over this for the better of the day, trying to recall any moment when I have known something like this kind of love. In prayer, in the depths of silence, there have been moments of great peace that often included fleeting sensations of an inward warmth and light. Once, in prayer on a desert retreat, sensations of warmth and light were especially strong. It was an experience, I realized, after the fact, in which there had been little if any distinction between pray-er and prayer. It also occurred to me that this "little death" of the self, and this sense of being wrapped in warmth and light, might just be a preview of what it was really like to die. And in that thought I found great comfort.

Still, my experience of a loving Presence seems so ethereal. If I am the one keeping my distance from a less ambivalent way of knowing this Presence in my life, how might I be more open? More attentive? As the day wears on, I begin to despair, feeling as though my experience of home in the landscape of the Spirit, if indeed I have experienced it at all, is hopelessly abstract.

Right around dinnertime, the storm breaks. I stick my head out of the tent, relieved to see patches of blue sky opening above Mount Emmons. I fire up the Coleman, boil some water, and cook up a packet of Cajun style red beans and rice—at eleven thousand feet, no less. Let the good times roll.

Out on the far side of the meadow, I notice a few elk edging out from the woods. It is a relief to be back in the open air. But my own dark thoughts still dog me. I carry them down to the little stream where I gather some water to clean my pot. And I carry them back to camp, into a little island of spruce and fir on the edge of the meadow.

Most of the blue has gone out of the sky. I stand near the edge of the trees washing the pot when I see something fly overhead. At first glance, it looks like a gray jay——one of those relatively fearless scavengers who like to glide into camp right around mealtime. But as I turn to walk back to the tent, the bird takes another pass, only a few feet over my head. Its wings are motionless. It leaves no sound in its wake. Its silhouette is as unmistakable as is a second, almost identical, saw-whet owl, which comes gliding in low from the opposite direction.

Now they both take a couple of passes, barely missing one another in flight as they circle over my head. I stand perfectly still, not wanting to scare them off. And for a while longer they circle, so quiet, so graceful, so low I reckon they are barely higher than the reach of my outstretched arm.

Finally, they fly off toward the stream and land in the dead branches of a storm-struck fir. Stunned, I stare at their perched silhouettes across the meadow. Then one, and then the other, swoop in toward me, this time gliding so low that their yellow eyes meet mine, each of them arcing up and away at the last possible instant.

POET GARY SNYDER DESCRIBES THE EGO AS LIVING ON THE EDGE OF that inward terrain where thought and imagination are beyond one's conscious control. The ego, he writes, occupies "a little cubicle somewhere near the gate" into this wilder mind, "keeping track of what goes in and out (and sometimes making expansionistic plots)." Beyond the gate, one's inward ecology takes care of itself. This is the soul's equivalent of a wild place.

I think of prayer as an invitation into the inward territory beyond the gate. I need to know that I can find that terrain of the spirit now and then, much as I need to know that this meadow is here, this old camp is here, that I can still find the hunter's place up a little higher, and that a walk along the ridgeline will allow me to really hear the wind again.

If the hunter was fortunate, he came home to the lower elevations with a wild offering to share with his family. Is it any different for wanderers and seekers? Any hunter will know periods of waiting when the game is scarce. So too, any seeker will pass through periods of waiting and listening and waiting some more, for some reassurance that he or she is on the right trail. Who is to say why this is so? Maybe it is a time of preparation so that one is able to receive something that is truly wild. Or so it occurs to me as I leave the meadow and my old camp behind and head down into the trees.

Later in the day, after a long-striding walk down the river trail toward the trailhead, I open that wooden gate again, close it behind me, and slide the horseshoe around that old fencepost. I think of a creek and a meadow. I think of a pile of chert on a high bluff. And I think that in the stillness of prayer and on the side of this mountain, the graces I know best have a way of moving on shortly after they arrive, not unlike a pair of sawhet owls on a slow glide into the last light falling.

Into the Big Empty

*"Spaciousness of soul—this is inner emptiness—the room
inside our hearts, the unfilled quality of consciousness
. . . Depending on how we meet this soul space, we may
experience it as open possibility or void nothingness, as
creative potential or dulling boredom, as quiet peaceful
serenity or as restless yearning for fulfillment."*

—Gerald May

June 19

WALKING IN A HIGH MEADOW IN THE HENRY MOUNTAINS, THROUGH
sagebrush and sparse grass, through an occasional ponderosa
pine shadow, toward an early morning sun already shining hard
on these east-facing slopes, I am checking out the "neighborhood." Charred pines below me trace the path a fire took, maybe
ten years back, judging from the young aspens that have grown
in thick along the northern edge of the meadow. Buffalo chips
every half dozen steps tell me this is one of the local herd's preferred habitats.

Under this wide Utah sky, the eye is tempted to wander.

Like the La Sals and the Abajos I can see out on the horizon
to my east, the Henrys are a pine-clad island of mountains in

the midst of canyonlands known simply to some old-timers as "the red country." Red, in this case, refers to a wide swath of color depending on the sandstone layer and the time of day. As my gaze falls back from those other mountain islands in the distance and across the canyons feeding the Dirty Devil River near the foot of the Henrys, burnt red turns orange, brown, tan, and then gray, as sandstones disappear under a layer of shale that is all but barren of plant life.

The Henrys ride the red country like the load on a pack horse. Ridgelines that begin in dwarfed forests of pinyon and juniper, run up to meet the sky, hitching these mountains to the surrounding high desert. The granite ridge to my west, still ribboned with snow, is lush and grassy by red country standards. At eleven thousand feet or so, the ridge is high enough to gather moisture from clouds that shed only shadows on the nearby town of Hanksville. A drop of Henry Mountain water might find its way down to those swerving lines of creek bed willows I can see trailing off into the canyons of the Dirty Devil out to the east, maybe even down to its confluence with the Colorado or beyond. But from this vantage point, the gray shale badlands at the base of the range look like a formidable obstacle.

I have come here with two stories on my mind. The first one has to do with two fugitives on the loose in southern Utah. They have been on the loose for ten days or so after shooting a policeman over by Dove Creek, Colorado. Described as survivalists, they are rumored to have ties with a militia group in the Four Corners area. One of the three, who surfaced in Bluff, Utah, shot himself as soon as the authorities closed in. Several hundred law enforcement people are still looking for the other two, who are known to have food caches throughout the Four Corners area.

As vast as southern Utah is, all the manhunt hype has me imagining a backcountry encounter with these survivalist desperados.

Some of the authorities believe they are holed up in a cave or maybe an old mineshaft in this part of Utah. All I know is that they are holed up in my imagination.

Yesterday, Grace and I drove over from Colorado, through the red dirt pinto bean farmlands around Dove Creek, west across the pinyon-juniper scrublands of Cedar Mesa, and farther west along the rim of White Canyon. Dropping down toward the shores of Lake Powell, we stopped for lunch at the Fry Canyon Café, an isolated outpost where the waitress told us she still felt edgy. The day before, she said, members of the search team had come through bearing Ak-47s.

In Hanksville, Utah, rangers at the Bureau of Land Management (BLM) office told us that food caches found near Lake Powell had prompted recent ground and aerial searches in the Henrys. Just a precaution, of course. There aren't many places in southern Utah that haven't at least been flown over. And there is an awful lot of country between the Henrys and the little town of Bluff where the other fugitive was found. Nevertheless, those other two guys are still on the loose. And they are still on my mind.

The other story I carry with me comes out of a different desert and a different time. It is the story of Jesus' forty day sojourn in the big empty of the Judean desert. Mark's gospel tells it this way: "And the Spirit *immediately* drove him out into the wilderness. He was in the wilderness forty days, tempted by Satan; and he was with the wild beasts; and the angels waited on him . . . ." I have been reading the Bible for the first time in a thorough way, and it occurred to me that maybe Jesus's story has something to teach me about my own attraction to solitude and out-of-the-way places. At the very least, it has encouraged me to see what it would be like to devote an extended wilderness retreat to prayer. Wilderness trips have always been restorative—helping me to come home to the present moment, to my body, to a quieter more contemplative "self"—-but I have never set out with the explicit intention of centering my time in prayer.

Mark says that the "Spirit immediately drove [Jesus] out into the wilderness." If my own decision to head out into the Henries was Spirit-led, my response was hardly immediate. In an especially restless period of my bookish life at seminary this past winter, the notion of a forty-day backcountry prayer retreat first surfaced on the pages of my journal. It felt like a reliable inward prompting. Conversations with trusted friends and mentors seemed to confirm that.

So I was willing to listen to this leading, and to act on it. But as my planned day of departure approached a few days ago, I couldn't even muster up the will to break away from the last two games of the NBA playoffs (a timely temptation and diversion). The underdog Utah Jazz had a shot at dethroning Michael Jordan and the Chicago Bulls, and as a devoted Jazz fan—a habit that I had developed living in Salt Lake City—I couldn't pass up the possible glory in that. The Henrys weren't going anywhere, I rationalized. And thirty-six days instead of forty, would still be plenty of time for a backcountry retreat. Maybe in the meantime those fugitives would get caught—-one less thing to worry about.

When the Jazz went down in the final seconds of the final game, the fugitives were still on the loose. And I was still feeling apprehensive. I'd done plenty of solo trips in the backcountry, but never for this long or for this reason. When we finally set out from our home base in Mancos, Colorado, I felt a hollow queasiness in my gut. But this was my window, and the opportunity for this kind of retreat might not come again any time soon.

So I wouldn't say I was "driven by the Spirit" to come out here. It felt more like an invitation—one that I have finally accepted. I have said goodbye to Grace. She will be back in a couple of weeks for a re-supply and a rendezvous. Other than that, I'm on my own. What I am planning to do, in the spirit of Jesus's sojourn (at least as I imagine it), is to stay put for five weeks or so—limiting myself to this mountain basin and the surrounding ridge and peaks (a place just as remote, though much less desolate, than his likely haunt in the Judean desert).

Limiting my physical territory and eliminating the need to move camp and cover miles will make my time here more spacious—spacious in the sense that it will be free of any tasks or obligations. I come here wanting the big empty, by which I mean spaciousness in place, in time, and in the wilder part of solitude and prayer, which this retreat will offer. But I am also afraid of it. Why? Maybe this sojourn, and maybe this gospel story, will help me find out.

The task at hand right now is to find an out-of-the-way camp—one that is secluded enough to serve as a hermitage for a month or so. Although this mountain basin has been grazed heavily by the buffalo herds that spend the summer months on the high slopes of this range, human tracks are scarce. As the mid-day glare obscures the canyons out east of the range, flies buzz through rising heat and winged grasshoppers crackle up then crash in their jerky mate-seeking flight. Even now, in mid-June, the sun is bright enough and strong enough to have me longing for shelter and shade and a camp near running water. But I have been looking for a while now, covering much of this alpine basin without finding that place, and the prospects are beginning to look a little grim.

Finding the right camp, I hope, will help relieve me of the dark imaginings that fill my thoughts. If it isn't the fugitives I am worried about, it is the possibility of being mistaken for one. I was reminded, before leaving Colorado, that I looked a little like one of the guys on the wanted posters. I was also reminded that there was good money being offered for their capture. So I made sure to let the BLM rangers in Hanksville know where I was going to be and that I was going to be there for a while.

I think of family voices back in Mancos: "Are you taking a cell phone? Are you traveling armed?" These are reasonable enough questions. I think of my father-in-law who usually carries a gun in the woods having once encountered an aggressive black bear. I think of a wildlife biologist up near Vernal who dialed out for help on his cell phone after being treed by a cougar. One could make a case for carrying a gun or a cell phone in the backcountry. But I have never been in the habit of "traveling armed." And the notion of taking a cell phone in the woods seems contrary to the intent of any backcountry adventure, let alone a retreat on which I intend to rely, as much as I can allow myself to rely, on the care of the Spirit.

As I drop down out of that dry meadow and begin to look for openings in a thick stand of young aspen, I can see the daylight of what appears to be a bigger clearing up ahead. But the hoped-for clearing turns out to be a slope dropping off into a heavily wooded ravine. I pause for a while. I listen to the sound of running water below me. And I follow it down through a thick stand of Douglas fir.

June 19 (Day One, Evening)

IF IT ISN'T THE SOUND OF THE WIND SIFTED THROUGH THE LONG needles of the ponderosa, it is the way the light falls through its branches that I find to be so welcoming. Here on this bench above the creek, shafts of late afternoon light slant down through a canopy of ponderosa branches. I feel sheltered here, but not hemmed in. I can still see plenty of sky.

Along with the reassuring sound of running water, the cascading notes of a hermit thrush drift down from the pine and aspen canopy. Sun flashes across the shiny tops of the aspens' shimmering heart-shaped leaves, then across their muted undersides as they are swept up in the breeze. Their flickering shadows dance across house-sized granite boulders, remnants of an igneous seam that runs through the ridge rising along the northern edge of this camp.

I hear a marmot whistle in the talus slope that begins on the far side of the creek to my south. Because of the talus and the ridge to my north, this place is hard to get to, even for a wide-ranging buffalo herd, traces of which can be found in the form of wallows and aspen tree scars (they like to run their horned heads against the aspen's smooth bark) almost everywhere in this basin except here.

I am hidden. It feels safe. So I spread out the tent in a clearing on the northeastern side of a small ponderosa and a couple of aspens, which I figure will shed some siesta shade my way in mid-day heat. The ground is slightly uneven, so I dig my hands into a layer of matted aspen leaves and lay them down in the low spots. To let in more of the sky, I set up the tent without pulling the fly across its mosquito net ceiling. It will be easy enough to opt for the fly if we get any weather.

Nearby I find a flat slab of sandstone that will make a good hearth. I empty a heavy nylon bag full of jerky and pasta, and about a month's worth of powdered soups and stews just to see it all laid out. Food is reassuring. Beside the hearth, I clear away the pine-needled duff and dig a small hole for a cooking fire. I light a bundle of pine needles that flare up around shreds of aspen bark and ponderosa twigs. Instant fire.

It is so windy here, and this forest is so dry and full of deadfall, it could torch up in a hurry. I intend to watch my fire closely, but what if someone else gets careless? There's no one else in this basin, I reassure myself. More likely to be lightning—no worries till it storms. Still, I can see how it would be possible to get trapped up in the basin. I think about wind patterns, about escape routes above timberline, about the talus slope on the far side of the creek, wondering if it could be a big enough refuge for waiting out a fire

It would be reasonable to spend time on these fire drill ruminations. But I continue to spin out the story web long after it has served any useful purpose—imagining dramatic wildfire escapes all the way through this first camp dinner of mac and cheese and on into the tent where I lie tangled up in my own fictions. I carry all sorts of wildfire scenarios into the twilight, well beyond the last trill of the hermit thrush that punctuates this day, and which will welcome me into morning.

June 20 (Day Two)

A PAIR OF GROSBEAKS WHO LIVE IN A DEAD PONDEROSA TRUNK JUST below camp have just chimed in with the hermit thrush—the cantor for these early morning "lauds." Chickadees . . . *chickadeedeedee* . . . and the chipping sparrows . . . *cheepcheep cheep* . . . fill in the chorus. I listen to them in cocoon mode—looking up from my sleeping bag into the brightening sky. Then I hear a hawk screech. And I see a big shadow flash through the branches. Sharp-shinned? Goshawk? Didn't get a good enough look, but the trees have gone songless.

I pull on a few layers and crawl out of the tent. The sun will soon be coming up from behind a mountain on the eastern edge of the Henries. I intend to greet it from the top of a big boulder—maybe fifteen feet high—I have scoped out as a morning prayer place. Tiny alcoves, which look a little like the "moki steps" carved into sandstone walls centuries ago by the Anasazi and Fremont people, make perfect toe and handholds for bouldering up the back wall of this morning rock. Up top, I pause to look over a wind, water, and ice-hewn depression in the rock—known in canyon country as a pothole—that holds a remnant from the last rain. And the water holds lots of wriggling larvae of one sort or another, not unlike the sea monkeys they used to sell on the back pages of comic books. Many of the tiny creatures that live in these potholes are capable of going dormant during dry spells, springing back to life after a good rain.

Little wonder that Jesus, being a desert dweller, likened the presence of the Spirit to "living water." Give us, this day, our living water. I settle myself on the big rock and take a few deep breaths. I imagine the inhale as that of God and the exhale as that in me I need to empty. I feel the rise in my chest with the new air and the settling of my lungs as the old air leaves. Then again. And then again.

Eyes closed now, I drift into a period of centering silence, feeling warmed in this newly-risen sun, and eventually, coming to rest on the aramaic word *maranatha*. Translated into the Greek as "Our Lord, come" or "Come Lord Jesus," the word carries echoes of ancient prayers. I think of it as an expression of my intention to be attentive and receptive. But the word isn't meant as a mantra. It isn't a dwelling place. It is more like a cairn on the path to an inward mountain, where maybe I can rest in an opening stillness.

Maranatha. Maranatha. Maranatha. While I am saying this word inwardly, I am greeted by a TV image that has seared itself into my psyche. I see Karl Malone, the great power forward for the Jazz, riding his Harley into the Delta Center before one of those final games against the Bulls. Karl comes. Karl goes, as do a collage of other random thoughts and images. And this is okay, I remind myself, as I let them pass. I let others pass. And gradually the lights slowly dim down in this great theatre of the mind.

In the moments of stillness that follow, I feel refreshed and nourished—a taste, perhaps, of that living water. But mostly what I feel is nothing at all. Nada, nada, and more nada.

A while later, I open my eyes. A doe and her fawn wander into view, walking underneath my perch on this big rock, their silent steps leaving no tracks in this leaf-covered clearing. They move warily though camp, looking ahead without seeing me looking down on them. And they disappear into scrub oak at the base of the ridge above me. I climb down from the boulder, gather up what I need from the hearth, and wind down through the big rocks and pines to find a place along the creek to get some water.

Down a pine-needled path under big ponderosas, I pass a rock alcove where a mother rock wren puffs out her feathers to shield three babies whose beaks are poking up over the edge of their nest. I walk past some old fir snags and into an opening in the creek bottom brush. On green mossy banks, next to a little pool dammed up by an old fir that spans the creek a few feet downstream, I lay out a tarp and sit down to begin what will become, like centering prayer on the boulder, a daily ritual.

As tedious as the task of pumping water through a filter may be, it is a good time to sit. And to look. Yellowjackets pause on the leaves of a bittercress patch just beginning to flower. A spider web, suspended over the creek, has snagged a wayward moth struggling to wing itself loose. Little flyers of some kind, barely bigger than dust motes, pass through pools of light and disappear into piney shadows. Poking out from the underside of the bank a feet away on the other side of the creek is a cluster of orange mushrooms.

Setting aside a few minutes for centering on the big rock and being still has settled my thoughts. Surely a part of prayer here is to leave that "small tent" where a soul can hole up—where it is possible to conceive of one's "self" as a thing apart—in order to walk into a sense of relationship with a much wider world. In *this* world, the ritual of pumping becomes a moment of thanksgiving. I gulp down an icy quart—drinking until I can no longer drink—filling myself with this Grace that runs fast and clear down the side of the mountain.

June 27 (Day Nine)

TODAY, I AM HEADING OUT TO LOOK FOR A FEW "WILD BEASTS"—- buffalo, in particular. Up the mountain, I find their tracks, hardened and cracked, as are the mudflat wallowing grounds in which the tracks were made. They must have left for higher ground some time ago. This herd benefits from changes in altitude, and therefore temperature, which the Henrys afford them. Varying elevations offer summer and winter pasture within a relatively short distance of one another. All the better that there are few fences in between, allowing the herd to range freely.

The trail that I walk now crosses the headwaters of the creek that runs past my camp and snakes up through some thick stands of fir and spruce to some high meadows on the ridge. For the buffalo, it is a thoroughfare between good grazing in the high meadows and the nearest source of water down below. Lately, it has been heavily traveled.

The trees are thick here. Very little morning sun finds its way down to the forest floor. I walk mostly in shadow. And I walk slowly around the blind curves on this trail. I smell buffalo as much as I smell fir and spruce, but I'm thinking it's less about their presence and more about what they've left behind. Ahead of me, a couple of firs have fallen across the trail. I am within fifteen feet of taking a detour around this deadfall when I hear a sudden snapping of branches on the far side. A huge bull of a buffalo lifts his great hulk into view. I can see the whites in his eyes as he cranes his massive skull toward me. My gaze and his gaze lock into one another. I am way too close and about to back off when he turns away and slams down through the tight spruce like a runaway truck. Several hundred feet down-slope in an aspen grove, he pauses, turning his big head back for one last look. Then he plods down toward the creek and disappears.

My heart pounds hard and fast. Grateful for the barrier that stood between us, I detour around the fallen trees and climb up through the remaining fir and spruce. Seeing sky through a stand of aspens, I am startled by a sound not unlike that of someone trying to start a chainsaw.

On the far side of this aspen grove, I can see a meadow that is full of clover and grasses and at least a dozen buffalo, mostly cows and calves, who graze quietly. Beyond them, there is a cloud of dust billowing up above the meadow. On the far side of a rise, a big bull rolls in the dirt, all the while grunting and groaning (and making that starting-a-chainsaw sound again) in the ecstasy of a good wallow. Another old bull lies in the clover along the edge of the meadow. He points his gaze my way . . . I think he has seen me peering out from behind this aspen tree. Then he goes back to munching on grass. A couple of year-lings spook as I dash from the shelter of one tree to another. They trot off through the meadow, warranting little more than a casual glance from their elders.

I continue to watch and listen for a while until the older bull on the edge of the meadow smells or sees me, perhaps for the second time, and decides I may be trouble. He rises to his feet. The rest of the herd does the same. He trots off and they follow. As they cross the meadow, and as the herd gathers its shape— the stronger cows and bulls folding in around the young and the vulnerable—they leave a cloud of dust in their wake. And the beating of their hooves gathers speed.

I watch until they have all run beyond the crest of the

ridge—glad for these moments, for a closer look at the kind of wildness in motion that finds a home in the Big Empty.

July 2 (Day Fourteen)

THE SKIN ON MY HANDS IS PARCHED AND CRACKING AS I WRITE THIS morning. This July sky has been filled with a great haze of yellow pollen, given off freely, in the heat wave of the last week or so, by the pines in this basin. My nostrils are dried out and filled with the stuff. Except in the cool of the mornings and evenings, the drone of flies is incessant. So I don't want to linger too long in camp today. But it is helpful to write.

Why solitude? It isn't about seeking any great mystical insight or developing some out-of-the ordinary contemplative skill. It just helps me to listen for an interior voice that is authentic and true and more likely to be found in stillness, than in the chaotic mix of voices I usually hear, both inwardly and outwardly, in the great flow of the day to day. It gives me a chance to "eddy out"—to spend a little time in the "still water" where reflection is possible. I don't think Jesus walked into the desert because he expected to find God; I think he went into solitude so that he could hear more clearly the Inward Teacher he brought with him.

For the last few days, I've been listening to questions that have no answers and I've been haunted by a sense of my own finitude and aloneness. For much of my life I've experienced moments when all temporal concerns fall away and I see myself and my immediate circumstance from a vantage point that is curiously detached. I am no longer thinking about the immediate circumstances of the moment at hand. I am aware only, for an instant, of its strangeness. What is strange is that there is a moment, or a person, or a place at all. This felt sense moves through me like a cold current through warm water. I am left floating in the wake of everything I can't know. Here, and maybe any place that is inwardly or outwardly empty enough, this sensation lingers. And so I am feeling weary in the presence of all the unanswerables. Meanwhile, prayer has been barren and empty. So I have been looking to the mountain for reassurance. This basin is two miles across from ridge to ridge (north to south) and about three miles across from the high peak west of my camp to the forest road that borders my territory on the east. Maybe a smaller space and a more confined daily routine would teach me more, as it apparently taught early desert monks who stayed put in their cells, but I doubt I would be up to that challenge. I am better at exploring the inward spaces that prayer and reflection seem to open, if I have room to wander on the outside. The tangible gifts that I find on this mountain—the shade of an aspen tree, a clear-running creek, waves of blooming wildflowers—are reassuring when prayer invites me into an experience of Presence that often *feels* more like absence.

I am ready for a break in the routine. I am ready for a break from these reflections. And I am eager to meet Grace down on the forest road in a few days. It will be good to turn my thoughts toward her and to share with her this place. I miss her. My small tent feels cavernous at night.

July 4 (Day Sixteen)

INDEPENDENCE DAY. GRACE AND I WALK THE HIGH RIDGE TOWARD the big peak west of camp. The wind has picked up. The air is no longer as heavy and sultry as it has been this past week. Above us, long and wispy mare's-tail clouds suggest that a change in the weather is on the way. Grace says it is the leading edge of a cold front.

Yesterday, we met down on the Forest Service road east of here and followed an old logging road back up to camp. I couldn't help but tease Grace about the jungle carbine rifle she was packing to soothe her concerns about potentially threatening predators (human or otherwise). Then again, who was I to second guess her needs or instincts?

So we both took comfort in being hidden below the steep talus and on the far side of the creek, where a new wave of lupines had flooded the bench land clearings with purple. A cool breeze blew across the flat pine-needled top of the boulder where we ate lunch and napped.

Later, on the other big rock——the rock that had become my perch for evening prayer——we read part of a psalm:

The Earth is the Lord's and all that is in it, the world, and those who live in it . . . Who shall ascend the hill of the Lord? And who shall stand in his holy place? (Ps. 24)

And we settled into a time of centering prayer——the silence somehow richer, as is often the case, in the presence of another person. A half hour later, opening our eyes to the last sliver of sun slipping away behind the big peak, Grace made a little cross out of twigs and grass and left it on the rock——a token of her blessing for this place and for the rest of my time here.

July 5 (Day Seventeen)

TODAY, WE WALK THE SWITCHBACKS ON THE TRAIL TO THE SUMMIT. I have been saving this trail and this summit to share with her. We criss-cross slopes that are covered with red clover and wrapped in a curious minty smell coming from some kind of alpine sage. I hear a raven caw and look up toward the summit. Two ravens approach, flying circles that occasionally intersect one another. Almost overhead, one tucks and dives and the other follows. They spiral down into the Douglas firs and out of sight.

On the summit, some climbers from Salt Lake have planted a

small American flag in a rock cairn. But there is no better tribute to independence than this raven's eye view of Navaho Mountain, Waterpocket Fold, San Rafael Swell, Book Cliffs, the Maze, Island in the Sky, the La Sals, the Abajos, Cedar Mesa—the heartlands of the Colorado Plateau that are spread out below us. For a few moments, in our slow turning from west to north to east to south and back to west again, and in the circle of a remembered prayer—*God before me, God behind me, God above me, God below me. I on your path. And you on mine*—we are, it seems, at the very heart of the big empty.

July 6 (Day Eighteen)

BACK DOWN AT THE TRUCK, WE HUG FOR A LONG TIME. AND HUG some more. Neither of us looks forward to another three weeks apart. I walk up the road, turn once to wave, and keep on walking. I hear Grace start the truck. Then I hear her driving off but can't look back.

Turning off the road and crossing the creek, I notice three yellow swallowtails on the edge of a mudflat. They slowly fan their wings as they drink from a shallow puddle. I watch them for a while. And I follow the flash of their yellow wings as they rise together like shards of sunlight into the dark clouds jutting up over the ridge.

Winding up through the pinyons and junipers and scrub oaks, the first set of switchbacks offer physical diversion enough to distract me from the sadness I feel over Grace leaving. Three more weeks of solitude feels less like a possible opening into prayer and more like a trail into desolation. I dread this walk. I have been dreading it ever since Grace got here. On this ascent, maybe I *am* "driven" by the Spirit. I'm not walking out of desire. I don't want this solitude now.

What is at the root of this dread? Thomas Merton talked

about two different levels of loneliness. Existential loneliness, he said, is at the core of the human condition. Beneath the web of relationship that connects us with others is the fundamental aloneness we experience in confronting our sufferings, and in approaching death. I am so bent on affirmation of my self, so steeped in the illusion that all my needs can be fulfilled, I rarely allow myself an experience of my own aloneness on this level. What I do experience, for the most part, is what Merton called anxiety loneliness—the dread of that deeper aloneness at the core of our being and the tension we feel when trying to avoid it. To walk into the terrain of existential loneliness, if only for a few moments at a time . . . is to leave behind the illusion I have no needs I cannot fill, that only a sense of relatedness to my Creator can address the loneliness beneath the loneliness I feel around Grace leaving. And yet that may be an opening in the midst of desolation—an invitation into deeper periods of reflection and prayer, much like Jesus experienced at the beginning of his sojourn.

But I am not ready for that now. The slate gray underbellies of the anvil clouds are building up over the ridge, telling me that the rain will soon come hard and fast. I have a wide meadow and an exposed talus slope yet to cross. And I am eager to get back to shelter. I can feel my breath racing as I begin to push the pace.

By the time I cross the old burn and drop down over the talus into the ravine, great gusts of wind shake the ponderosas and bend the aspens eastward. I crawl into the tent as the first sheets of rain wash over the fly. And I burrow into my sleeping bag—counting the seconds between lightning flashes and the sharp cracks of thunder that echo off the surrounding peaks and ridges. I think about all the old trees on this hillside, wondering which, if any, will draw a bolt. Shrinking intervals between the light and the sound tell me that the heart of the storm is still headed my way.

The storm rides along the rim of this mountain basin. About the time I think it has run its course out over the ridge to my east, another round of thunder rumbles down off the mountain to my west. Moments later, a flash, then a crack that seems to shake this ground. I burrow deeper into my bag as if making myself invisible will shield me from the bolt, I worry, is headed my way.

July 12 (Day 24)

IN MORNINGS AND EVENINGS BEFORE CENTERING PRAYER, I'VE BEEN reading the psalms, many of which have offered me comfort over the last few days. Why? I feel less isolated when I read the psalmist's words of despair in feeling so small or so distant from God. And I feel less isolated in my own orientation toward experiencing the holy (that being, for the most part, an outdoor one) when I find, throughout the psalms, references to God as rock and refuge: "My God, my rock in whom I take refuge" (Ps. 18); "Lead me to the rock that is higher than I; for you are my refuge" (Ps. 61); "My mighty rock, my refuge is in God" (Ps. 62); "The Lord lives! Blessed be my rock. (Ps. 18)." Reading these psalms facing west toward the mountain that defines the western boundary of this wayfaring ground, brings the scripture into this place and this place into the scripture.

This morning, I find a prayer nested in the forty-third Psalm, and I take it up the mountain: *Send out your light and your truth; let them lead me; let them bring me to your holy hill and to your dwelling.*

Patches of blue penstamons light up the pine-needled ground on the way down to the creek where I pause, splash my face, clean the lenses of some cheap shades held together with ducttape, and head up toward the talus. I hear a marmot whistle up in the boulders ahead of me. And I surprise one of its burly offspring sunning on top of a nearby rock. It is hard, even for a baby "whistle pig," to flatten himself out enough to become invisible, but this little guy is intent on trying as I walk by.

Up top of the talus, I take a look out east—it is so hazy that I can barely see the La Sals and Abajos. There is still a distant plume of smoke rising up from Cedar Mesa—somewhere up around Natural Bridges. In a register up on the mountain, a recent entry says something about fires down on the Arizona strip, which may be contributing to the haze. Even with the recent storms, it is still mighty dry.

But the wildflowers are coming on strong. Indian paintbrush and skyrocket gilia splash red along the edges of the old burn. Patches of wild roses bloom between clumps of mountain mahogany. Yellow daisies cover the ground wherever the fire or the buffalo or both have been. Along an old logging trail, I run across a spindly white yarrow, a few dried up asters, and a lone sego lily—that white chalice of a flower, orange-eyed on the inner petals, whose bulbs were a staple for Mormon pioneers and for the native inhabitants who preceded them.

The best find of all are two white columbines—the first I've seen in the Henrys. With long tails trailing off behind brilliant white petals, the columbines look like flowering comets. I bend down for a closer look and offer up a little praise: "You two are looking mighty fine." It has been ten days or so since I have uttered a word. My voice sounds as though it belongs to someone else.

Send out your light and your truth; let them lead me; let them bring me to your holy hill and to your dwelling.

The route to the high ridge runs up a steep spur. The more I climb it, the more I contour along a bulge in the slope about two thirds of the way up, the more like an owl's beak it seems to me.

Birds of prey, though not as plentiful as I expected they might be in this mountain basin, are usually heard, if not seen, as I make my way up the beak. On this particular morning, some sparrows are pestering a marsh hawk, which is passing through on an upslope draft.

Threading my way up through the firs and aspens on the crest of the beak, I follow deer trails braiding in and out of one another. I circle around a big fir when one of its branches explodes into a flurry of wings. Like a whack on the shoulder from a Zen-master, sage grouse says, "Wake up!" A little further up the beak, I surprise a three-point buck that sees me and snorts a warning. A glint of sun falls on the velvet of his antlers as he springs through the trees. There is some buffalo sign up this way, but the beak is deer country. Back in camp, I have scoped them with binoculars from the evening rock as they venture out beyond the trees and into the high meadows at the end of the day.

Walking the beak each morning, I see the bent-grass circles where they bed down the night before. Being present to such details is part of the prayer in walking for me. This is mountain scripture, I think, as I read the passage of a deer trail and follow it up to the treeline.

Send out your light and your truth; let them lead me; let them bring me to your holy hill and to your dwelling.

Bristlecone pines grow where the wind blows hard. In the sylvan community, they are the old eccentrics living out on the edge of the village. Here, the branches of the most exposed bristlecones look as though they are reaching out to latch on to the tail of the wind as it blows by. One bristlecone, which looks as though it must be at the vortex of a perennial whirlwind, has branches headed in opposite directions, wrapping around one another and around a twisted trunk, as if the tree is shielding itself from the elements, or maybe holding itself in place.

About two thirds of the way up the beak, at the top of a steep rocky pitch, I stop to rest beside a favorite bristlecone. It would take at least three tree-huggers to ring the base of this trunk. I sit down beside a twisted root—one of a half-dozen or so that anchors the trunk to the rocks and boulders that surround it. It is as big and as smooth as a human thigh.

Like most of the tree, this root has been stripped of bark. How long ago, I wonder? A century? A millennium? And how? Was it a porcupine? Or a lightning strike? I know it is due in part to the relentless work of wind and ice. Bristlecones like this one are slow to grow and slow to die. If I could see this tree in cross-section, I would see that the growth rings are especially dense in this twisted trunk which is what protects this tree from insect parasites and fungi.

There are bristlecones out in the Great Basin that are four thousand years old. Hereabouts, they are less ancient. This one is probably about two thousand years old. I lay my hand on the root, then slide my palm along the skin-smooth wood as it curves into the ground. And I slide it back again. And then I pause for a moment or two in prayer—nothing elaborate, just a moment to say thanks and to express the hope that this tree, here perhaps in the form of a seedling right around the time that Jesus went off into the desert, will be around for my children and their children and their children to rest beside.

I feel a little foolish as I mutter this prayer. But with every word, I feel less so. What I feel most in prayer is vulnerable. And that feels right. I think of it as part of the tendering that softens hard places in the heart. And opens a way into the spaciousness where love can grow.

Send out your light and your truth; let them lead me; let them bring me to your holy hill and to your dwelling.

The wind lives out past the last of the trees. Even on sultry July days like this one, there is a breeze along the high ridge. Most of the time, it comes out of the west, falling down from the piney highlands of Boulder Mountain, across a snake's spine of sandstone called Waterpocket Fold, across the desolate hills and mesas of the gray shale, up through the open sagebrush country to the western edge of the Henries, through the scrub oaks and pinyon-juniper forests, out into the high meadows where the buffalo like to graze, and up to a ridge between rounded peaks, where I sit looking toward a caucus of crows—dark speckles on a band of snow which lies like a new moon on the crest of the ridge.

Each morning, rising winds bring out the bigger birds—once a golden eagle, sometimes goshawks, more often redtails and marsh hawks—for a little freewheeling. That means mostly tilting and tail-feather ruddering, only a wing beat or two to the mile as they float along the crest of this long ridge. Crows and ravens are the thermal club regulars. The crows patrol the ridge in larger packs (usually a half dozen or so). I hear their raucous chatter as they pass overhead. The ravens prefer to fly solo or with a partner.

As I sit in the grass, just east of the ridgeline, a bumble bee zips by overhead and rides the west wind into an updraft, headed for a vanishing point in flat-bottomed clouds that carry the reds from the canyons below. For a few moments the air is still. Then another wind wave breaks across the crest of the ridge, carrying a swallowtail that has just lit out from a red clover blossom. It is gone a hundred feet before it moves a wing. Adios angelito.

Although the westerly wind comes and goes, it is prevalent much of the time, if only in a slight breeze blowing up high. Thermals and downdrafts are more cyclical. When the weather is stable and clear, the thermals rise with the sun along both slopes of the range. The downdrafts go the other way shortly after dusk.

I breathe in and out slowly, savoring this moment, this place, much as I have savored the lines of the psalm I brought with me today. In the slow and deep reading of scripture known as *lectio divina* (sacred reading), extended periods of revery and imagination are welcomed. In the lectio of this moment and this place, it isn't much of a stretch to imagine myself breathing inside of the great inhale—-the winds that rise with the sun that carries the taste of sand and sage up the mountain. Nor is it hard to imagine an exhale riding the night wind down, somewhere out to the east of the Henries.

July 19 (Day Thirty-one)

ONE OF THE OLD STORIES TOLD ABOUT THE HENRIES HAS TO DO WITH a statue of Jesus. Legend has it that the statue was eight feet long and made of solid gold. It had been cast in New Mexico and was bound for a mission in California, along with altar vessels and several smaller statues of the Virgin Mary. After a successful crossing of the Colorado River, the westbound caravan attempted navigate the Henries. Some accounts say there was an Indian attack. Others say the wagon that was carrying the statue fell apart in rough terrain. All versions of the story say that the·statue was buried up here.

Used to be, this story was told around campfires in southern Utah and northern Arizona. Mormon families who settled the region passed the story down from one generation to the next. Some people took the story to heart and came into the Henries determined to locate the treasure. One account, somewhat sketchy in detail, told of three young prospectors who found traces of an old trail heading into the Henries. Deep in the heart of this range, they found part of what they were looking for and emerged some weeks later with a Virgin Mary eight inches long and a bowl ten inches in diameter, both of which were made of gold.

The golden Jesus tale has the ring of the classic lost mine stories told all over the west, especially in places like the Henries, which are remote and a little on the desolate side.

The big empty seems to attract such stories, much as it once attracted the yondering prospectors who were seeking out the last best places where some "good color" or an untapped vein might still be found.

In Matthew's gospel, Jesus says, "He who loses his life for my sake will find it." Such an outlook would have encouraged a very different approach to walking the big empty—one that was less about finding something and more about losing it. But losing what, exactly?

I wonder about this under a night sky that is graced with only a sliver of moon. The stars are especially brilliant tonight. I have been lying here long enough to see Signus the Swan slide across the opening in the aspen-ponderosa canopy above my tent. It is late. Too late to be pondering such things. Too late . . . to be wondering what, if anything, I have may have lost or gained out here over the last month or so. But I am wondering, nevertheless.

I have read in Luke's gospel that Jesus returned after his forty days, "filled with the power of the Spirit." He came home having succeeded in denying those obstacles that the tempter (aka Satan) presented. The way I read the story, his struggle with temptation was an inward one. He said no to that inward voice that promised comfort and security, no to the offer of power and adulation, and no to the offer of controlling his own destiny. Instead he chose to listen for a deeper inward voice, a deeper authority.

And that has been my intent in prayer out here—to listen for deeper currents I am unable to hear when I am too concerned about my own security, too needy of the reassurances and affections of others, too intent on maintaining an illusory sense of my own power and control, too caught up in my own narratives to realize that I am living inside of a much bigger story. In the spaciousness of the big empty—whether an outward geography or an inward one—I can take "a long, loving look at what's real," as Teresa of Avila once put it.

I wonder how Jesus's life would have been different if there had been no big empty—no wild place for a forty day sojourn . . . or later, no wild place for him to pray apart from his followers. Something to ponder back at seminary, I guess. No need to get too theological tonight. There are other more immediate questions. Like: What the heck is that noise?

It is a guttural grunting kind of a sound. And it seems to be coming from up top the talus, maybe a quarter mile from camp, though at times it sounds much closer. I think of bear. I recall the strange heavy breathing sound I once heard beyond the wall of my tent up in the Wind River Range. I finally managed to rustle up enough gumption to poke my head out the tent and shine a light on the beast thinking that at least I'd know what I was dealing with. Turned out, I never saw it. But judging from the branches I heard snapping as it loped off through the woods, it must have been a black bear on the prowl.

So now my late night thoughts in the Henrys return to black bear, even though I know that the sound is coming from what has been in the past a popular buffalo bedding ground. If it is a bear, how big is it? Is it headed this way? Is it just my imagination or is that sound getting a little closer? Maybe it is my imagination. Or maybe it's just buffalo.

July 20 (Day Thirty-two)

DAYBREAK FINALLY COMES AFTER A FEW HOURS OF FITFUL SLEEP. I have come to the end of a three-day fast and breakfast is on my mind. I wash a little jerky down with a cup of coffee and have a few dried apricots for dessert. Having almost forgotten about those strange night sounds, I hear rocks sliding down the talus slope.

Something or someone is headed my way. I know it isn't buffalo. Buffalo hooves don't work well on steep rocky ground like that. Who or what else would be coming down those rocks? After thirty-some days, I admit I've come to feel more than a little territorial about this camp. I run over to the evening rock where a break in the trees affords me a better view and where I may catch a glimpse of the "intruder." Then again, it might be Grace coming in a day early, but I am too late to find out. Who or what just came down the talus has disappeared. I watch for movement in the trees down below. Nothing. So I go back to the hearth for another cup of coffee.

Time passes. No further sign of movement out yonder. I wander down the bench—-in part to walk off the uneasiness I'm feeling about this unsolved mystery. Above me, the regulars are out and about: chickadees, juncos, Clark's nutcrackers, and a flock of pygmy nuthatches. I hear a towhee. And I am trying to scope out a flash of yellow I saw up in the aspens, when I hear a large branch snap a few hundred feet up the hill behind me.

As I turn, I hear another branch break and I see the tail end of a young black bear, looking almost blonde in the morning sun as it lopes through a clearing in the aspens. Looking back over its shoulder once, it rambles up toward the scrub oak. I watch until I see the last of the scrub oaks shaking.

That must be what I heard on the talus, I'm thinking, and maybe what I heard last night. Then again, whatever that was last night sounded a whole lot bigger than I imagine a young bear sounding. Maybe there is another bear hereabouts.

Back at camp, I hang the food bag higher and a further away from the tent. And then it occurs to me that maybe I should be moving on. It wouldn't hurt to grant that bear some territory. Besides, I've been in this spot for more than a month and

I may be getting too territorial myself. Time to let the locals have their home back. It will be good to spend my last few nights up high.

I remember a nice bivouac site up on the beak. So I pack up my stuff and no-trace the place, leaving Grace's little cross on one of the evening prayer rocks. I pause for a few moments of silent thanks at the hearth, at the tent site, and at each of the prayer rocks, and I walk down to the creek to do the same by the pool where I drew my water each morning. Then comes the big schlepp up the beak. Meanwhile, the front edge of a new storm front comes drifting in over the big peak.

July 22 (Day Thirty-four)

FOR THE LAST FEW DAYS, UNSETTLED WEATHER HAS LIMITED MY travel time to mornings up here on the beak. But yesterday I was able to get back to a meadow over on the far side of the mountain. There, I learned something new about the buffalo. I had just emerged from a stand of Doug Fir when I came up on the herd unexpectedly. A couple of old bulls posted as sentries saw me coming and snorted an alarm to the rest of the herd, who were bedding down nearby. I'd heard that sound before. In fact, I'd spent most of a night listening to it.

I began to visualize the cause of the commotion that had kept me up that night at my old camp. I imagined the young bear showing up late—an appearance that surely would have riled up the old sentry bulls, hence the strange sounds from the top of the talus. The buffalo eventually took off for higher ground, while the young bear stayed around and came down my way after daybreak. Seems I hadn't been the only one to cede a little territory to a wandering bear.

This morning the weather broke for a while. I got up before daybreak, just before it clouded up again, and saw the lights of

Hanksville off in the distance. Another twenty-four hours and Grace will be here. Today I will move camp down toward the road so that I can be there waiting when she arrives.

July 23 (Day Thirty-five)

I STAND UNDER A SCRUB OAK IN A DRIVING RAIN, CLOSE ENOUGH TO the road to see yet another unfamiliar truck headed up the road toward a circle of RVs that have staked out turf for a Pioneer Day Family Reunion. It begins to rain even harder. The oaks give pretty good cover. And inside of all my rain gear I am fairly dry—comfortable enough to stay put, to watch the rain drip down from the leaves overhead and to enjoy the spectacle of an occasional lightning flash. I look up toward the mountain, but can only see part way up the beak. The clouds have swallowed up my bivouac camp and shrouded the big peak.

What with the spectacle of the storm and the prospect of Grace driving the old Ford up the road to meet me, I am feeling festive. Then a troubling thought wedges its way into the moment. What if the road turns gumbo somewhere down in the shale and she isn't able to make it up the mountain? I have a gloomy vision of myself, drenched and dejected, holding my bowl out like Oliver Twist at the Mormon family feed up the road.

Another truck passes and the thought fades. The rain seems to be letting up. Still, it is coming down hard. While I listen to the cadence of the rain as it sweeps across the basin along with great gusty winds when, the melody of "Wild Thing" comes to mind. I imagine Jimi Hendrix pounding out the cords:\ ". . . *rai-rrr-nairrh-nairrh-nairrh-nairrh-nairhh-nairhh* . . .". Inwardly, I sing along with that line in the refrain: "Wild Thing (*rairrr-nairrh-nairrh-nairrh-nairrh*) You make my heart sing . . ."

I've heard the song many a time, but this time I hear it as a psalm with some serious voltage behind it. I imagine a Stratocaster and a wall of amps, and shrieking feedback. Even the cadence of the rain picks up to go along with this soundtrack that has me smiling like a fool in the midst of the downpour.

It isn't long before I see our white Ford barrel around the bend. The rain has let up, and a shaft of light has broken through a hole in the shroud that has all but covered the mountain. It is a good thing that I have walked down the road a ways to meet Grace, because as it turns out, she does get stuck, right there on the hill below my scrub oak shelter.

No matter. We back the truck down a ways, pull off to the side of the road, and in our wild jubilation, amidst all the hugs and smiles and such, we unpack a lunch of cheese and crackers, and fresh cherries Grace picked up at a roadside stand in Monticello. I am trying to explain the giddiness I felt, standing out there in the rain with that "Wild Thing" refrain of a mantra. She nods and smiles as if such behavior is to be expected from someone who has been out in the woods and on his own just a little too long.

July 24 (Heading home)

THE FOLLOWING MORNING, AFTER AN EVENING OF TELLING STORIES, catching up on news (the two other fugitives, I find out, are still on the loose,) and cuddling up around a ponderosa fire, we are driving down the road toward Hanksville. I think back on the last few weeks of my time out here, still savoring that deluge in the scrub oaks. If the inward way or "the night way" of prayer is the way of emptying into that wildness beyond all words and images, the outward way seeks the Holy in all of creation— whether in the Bible or in the scripture of place. I need both ways of prayer in order to be fully open to those "wild thing" moments of joy.

God's first language is silence, I heard Father Thomas Keating say, and indeed that has been true in my experience. But Thomas Kelly also likened the movement of the spirit in one's life to a kind of "holy whispering"—and that rings true as well, not in the sense that I have actually heard any voices out here, but rather that I came here in response to the "whisper" of something akin to a deeply held and slowly emerging intuition.

In the past, I have harbored, however unconsciously, an ideal of transformation suggesting that time spent in the big empty—in those widest of spaces in prayer or in place—would somehow relieve me of my shortcomings. Could it be that the big empty experience of my own aloneness and incompleteness is just as valuable? What if the beauty I associate with wholeness and fulfillment is also present in the emptiest inward terrain, where the deepest of my longings for the Spirit are rooted? Am I ready now to let go of the myth that says I should never feel empty or unfulfilled? If there has been a losing and a finding for me here, can I bring it home today in these queries that I carry? Best to let it all season for a while.

That's what feels right as we ride the switchbacks down through the shale and out onto the sagebrush flats. Out in the distance to the north, I can see that line of cottonwoods where Hanksville should be. In the rearview mirror, I can see that the big peak west of my old camp is still socked in. All around us, the previous night's rain has soaked the sage. I roll down the window and that old sagey fragrance is everywhere. I take a long breath and let it go. I take another, deeper still, and I begin to let it out again.

In God's Wildness

Oquirrh Range, Utah

"In God's wildness lies the hope of the world."

—John Muir

"Can you lift up your voice to the clouds,
so that a flood of waters may cover you?
Can you send forth lightnings, so that they may go
and say to you, 'Here we are'?
Who has put wisdom in the inward parts,
or given understanding to the mind?"

—Book of Job 38:34-38

WHEN JOHN MUIR TALKED ABOUT GOD'S WILDNESS, HE MAY NOT
have had the Oquirrh Mountains in mind. But the letters he
wrote during a ramble through northern Utah back in 1877
suggest that's what he experienced there. I was thinking about
those letters as I drove west out of Salt Lake City toward the

Oquirrhs, pondering his notion that wildness, hope, and God were all bound up in one another.

In the distance, spreading across more and more of my windshield as I crossed Redwood Road heading west, was the El Capitan of mining heaps—a high coppered slope that rimmed the world's largest man-made hole. I had heard that only two human creations were visible from outer space: one was the Great Wall of China, the other was Kennecott's open pit copper mine up Bingham Canyon.

God's wildness seemed an abstract concept as mile after mile of urban strip slipped by and King Copper loomed larger ahead. But for John Muir, who stood along the banks of the nearby Jordan River, listening to "the still small voice of flowers at his feet" and "studying the darkening sky" above what was then a wide open valley, God's wildness was as real as a storm that he watched sweep in off the Great Salt Lake a few miles to the north:

> At 4:30 PM, a dark brownish cloud appeared close down on the plain towards the lake, extending from the northern extremity of the Oquirrh Range in a northeasterly direction as far as the eye could reach . . . . In a few minutes it came sweeping over the valley in wild uproar, a torrent of wind thick with sand and dust, advancing with a most majestic front . . . . Scarcely was it in plain sight, racing across the Jordan, over the city, and up the slopes of the Wasatch, eclipsing all the landscapes in its course—the bending trees, the dust streamers, and wild onrush of everything movable giving it an appreciable visibility that rendered it grand and inspiring.

The gale continued for another hour or so. The "blessed" wind, rain, and snow that followed in its wake "filled the whole basin

. . . bestowing . . . benefactions in most cordial and harmonious storm measures." For Muir, this was cause for celebration.

If his delight in reading the "scripture" of place had opened him up to an experience of wildness, how would he read this landscape now? Lower, drier, and scrubbier than the shining peaks of the Wasatch Mountains across the valley, the Oquirrhs were known mostly as a range that had been fenced off and worked over. If they weren't written off because of little if any public access, they were regarded, less charitably, as a corporate wasteland. The same mountains that Muir had described as "the Range of Lilies" because of the incredible flower specimens he found there, I associated not only with Kennecott's big pit copper mine, but also with the Mercur Mine on the southern end of the range, where the cyanide method for extracting gold had been invented; with the chemical weapons incinerator a little further south, known to have released nerve agent into the atmosphere; with plumes of chlorine and hydrochloric acid drifting in from the infamous Magnesium Corporation to the northwest of the range.

Heading into the town of Bingham, the high rim of the pit loomed dead ahead. Up the main drag, I drove past the school, company homes, a boarded up café, and a defunct mining museum. Driving into the canyon above town, it looked as though I was headed into the pit itself. Then the road looped back and up, climbing steep slope switchbacks toward the visitor center. Below me, trucks as big as houses were hauling away Oquirrh Mountain ore. Beyond the pit to the west, scrub oaks shaded the mountain slopes red. Further up, curving bands of sedimentary rock rippled through the Oquirrhs, evidence of the folds and faults that had helped to shape the range. Higher still, tawny meadows of subalpine grasses sheathed the high ridges, which occasionally crested, as if rolling in off the Great Salt Lake, into snow-capped peaks.

A while later, I sat in the Visitor Center's darkened theater with a busload of Japanese tourists, watching an interpretive film that featured a hard-hatted, blue-collared, Hollywood-slick film narrator who spewed out statistics about the size of the hole, the amount of ore produced, the engineering logistics, and the global appetite for copper.

The image of a full-sized pick-up driving into the bucket of a massive front-end loader seemed to make the biggest impression on this particular audience—inspiring an audible sigh of amazement. Then the lights came on and the curtains on the wall behind us parted, revealing a huge picture window and the spectacle of the world's largest man-made hole below us. Roads spiraled down to the bottom of the pit where the same house-sized trucks I had passed on the way up, now looked like Tonka Toys.

"Lovers of science, lovers of wildness, lovers of pure rest will find here more than they may hope for," Muir wrote in a simpler more optimistic time. One hundred and twenty-five years later, it was hard to conceive of the Oquirrhs as a haven of wildness, let along a place of "pure rest."

WILDNESS, AS I HAD COME TO UNDERSTAND IT, WAS FULL OF PARA-dox. It was at once a quality that we feared and one that we were drawn to. If it described a place, one might think of terrain that was uncultivated, uninhabited, maybe even desolate. One might also imagine a place where the native flora, fauna, as well as the human spirit, were free to flourish.

I pulled off the highway near the northern tip of the Oquirrhs and drove by the Moorish pavilion that stands by itself, gold-domed and surreal, on the edge of the Great Salt Lake. Now a tourist stop, Saltair was a relic of the original dance hall and amusement park that John Muir likely would have noticed as he rolled out to Lakepoint on the train back in 1877. I drove a little further and parked near a shallow bay. Late in the summer, the gulls were gliding in over their own reflections in mudflat pools, and the air had that stagnant dead sea smell that often lingers along the shore of the lake.

Muir wrote of his first swim here, back in the days when tourists stayed at a hotel and resort that would have been a mile or two off to the west. That hotel was long gone. Few folks ventured into the lake anymore. Fewer still wandered up into the northern peaks of the Oquirrhs (now Kennecott property). Shortly after his immersion in the waves that were rolling in off the lake that day, Muir imagined himself walking those high Oquirrh ridges off to the south "bathing in the high sky, among cool wind waves of snow . . . . Now," he wrote, "I shall have another baptism."

For John Muir, the world was sacramental. Anything anywhere, especially anywhere wild, was capable of revealing or reflecting a Divine Presence. A mountain ramble was no less capable of becoming an act of worship than the rituals of baptism and communion. He was able to draw on religious language to describe his experience. Scripture offered Muir a context in which to place the holiness of his experience, though it was his experience of place and Spirit that came first.

The theology of wild places that he began to articulate in some of his early mountain essays did not sit well with his father, a dark-tempered Calvinist preacher. "You cannot warm the heart of the saint of God with your cold icy-topped mountains," wrote Daniel Muir in a furious rebuttal to his son's writings. " . . . Come away from them to the spirit of God and his holy word, and he will show our lovely Jesus unto you . . . the best and soonest way of getting quit of the writing and publishing of your book is to burn it, and then it will do no more harm either to you or others."

John Muir learned the Bible under threat of his father's whip. His mother Anne taught him to read the scripture of place. She introduced him to the strawberries that grew underneath the meadow grasses, the robins that filled the oak groves with their high lilting song, and the fireflies that sprinkled light into the sultry summer evenings on their Wisconsin farm. John Muir's sense of the Spirit was seeded in those moments of beauty and grace that his mother helped him to see. Whether in the waves of the Great Salt Lake or in the lilies that he would find later that day in the snow fields of the Oquirrhs, divine ministry, he would come to believe, was everywhere.

"We seem to imagine that since Herod beheaded John the Baptist, there is no longer any voice crying in the wilderness," Muir wrote. " . . . God's love covers all the earth as the sky covers it, and also fills it in every pore. And this love has voices for all who have ears to hear."

Muir was better than most at paying attention and as fervent as anyone in spreading his mountain gospel. In a strident burst of mountain evangelism, he once approached a "grave old Mormon" in Salt Lake with whom he'd been having theological discussions, brandishing some newly collected specimens from the Oquirrhs: "I shook my big handful of lilies in his face, and shouted, 'Here are the true saints, ancient and Latter-Day, enduring forever.'"

HEADING WEST FROM SALTAIR, I DROVE THE GEOGRAPHICAL ALLEY-way between the great expanse of the lake to the north and the steep northern face of the Oquirrhs to the south. Rounding the edge of the Oquirrhs, the Great Basin opened up in all its desolate and holy splendor. To the west and north were the low desert hills and salt flats, and beyond that, the long straight road to Nevada, where the occasional highway mileage sign offered only superficial orientation in a geography too wide and vast to fully comprehend.

Ten or fifteen miles off to the southwest, the Stansbury Mountains edged in a valley, as the Oquirrhs did on the east, bringing a little more scale and definition to this piece of the high desert. For those living in valley towns like Tooelle and Grantsville, both ranges offered shelter —from Salt Lake's urban sprawl to the east and from the alkaline and more inhospitable desert further to the west. The Oquirrhs also provided a psychological buffer for folks living in Salt Lake City, making it easier to forget that one was living on the other side of the mountain from a seemingly placid valley that was also home to a chemical weapons incinerator and to Magcorp, one of America's most notorious corporate polluters. Tooelle County had been described as the most toxic place in America.

I turned off the Interstate, passing through a couple of gas stations and fast food joints. Heading south, Highway 36 was heavy with traffic. Despite the geographical barrier of the Oquirrhs, despite the area's toxic reputation, towns like Tooelle and Grantsville were attracting new settlers, many of whom commuted in and out of Salt Lake's urban sprawl. Irrigated fields along the highway were growing subdivisions faster than alfalfa.

If Tooelle County was so toxic, why would anyone want to move there? Partly because the sun came up behind one mountain range and set behind another. Snow-capped ridges caught the light and let it go again, as did the great blue sweep of the lake off to the north. Red-winged blackbirds chattered along ditches that brought water to farms and ranches on the outskirts of town. In quiet neighborhoods off the main drag in Tooelle and Grantsville, senior citizens tended to their lawns and flowerbeds, moms wheeled babies in sidewalk strollers, and kids rode their bikes down wide tree-lined streets.

Historically, the agricultural economy in towns like Tooelle and Grantsville, like the mining economy in Bingham Canyon, had had its booms and busts. As in many parts of the country, relentless heat, drought, and wind blew in one of the worst busts back in the 1930s. Many family farms and ranches went under. A decade or so later, the army came in and built a depot. Locals welcomed them as they would the Magnesium Corporation a few years later. A steady supply of jobs with benefits meant a lot in a marginal economy. If, over time, there were environmental risks—living next to half of the country's stockpile of chemical weapons, for example, or breathing toxic fumes while working at Magcorp—they were either unknown or ignored. When the risks of weapons incineration and industrial pollution came to light later on, there were those who still chose to disregard them.

But Tooelle County had paid a price for any economic benefits received. In 1996, an organization called West Desert HEAL (Healthy Environment Alliance), founded by librarian Chip Ward and a handful of Grantsville residents concerned about community health, conducted a survey. In interviews with around 2,500 residents, about half of Grantsville's population, they found what many had long suspected: an usually high incidence of cancer, respiratory ailments, and birth defects, among other things. Several HEAL members, Ward among them, were so concerned about the health of their community that they considered relocating their families. But contacts with other community activists confronting similar situations, some in remote areas, convinced Ward that you could run, but you could not hide.

Later that afternoon, from a perch about halfway up a sliver of BLM land on the western slope of the Oquirrhs, I could see a high yellowish plume rising up from the stacks at the Magcorp Plant on the far western edge of the Great Salt Lake. A breeze blowing in from the lake and up from the valley floor carried a hint of that sulphury mudflat smell. I also caught a whiff of something like Clorox in the air as well—a fairly common occurrence when the wind was blowing in from Magcorp's direction. Closer at hand, curled up on a flat rock, I noticed the yellowed coil of an old snakeskin. It was so light and brittle that a puff of wind broke off a piece of the tail end. Light filtered through the scales as I held the rest of it up against the sky. Though I'd been on the lookout for rattlesnakes on previous climbs up here, especially while scoping out hand-holds on routes up through the limestone, this was the closest I had come to one.

I dropped down a gully and began the long trek up through the scrub oaks. It had been a dry summer. Contouring across patches of grass in between clumps of oak, old mules' ear stalks crunched underfoot. Some months back, a small fire had run its course up this slope, leaving behind streaks of charred and leaf-less scrubland. Already, bright red patches of Indian paintbrush lit up the blackened ground.

Finding routes through the oaks, especially when they grew as thick as they did on the western slopes of Oquirrhs, was a matter of winding this way and that, always moving toward the openings so as to avoid the stiff, knobby branches that gave you a thrashing if you gave them half a chance. But on the steep grade below limestone escarpments, those same stubborn scrub oaks made pretty decent hand-holds. I tugged on one as I entered a gravelly chute up through a break in the cliff, followed a few twists and turns that led me up to the foot of an old juniper—one of those wind-worn hermits making a life out there on the edge. I passed several specimens of curl-leaf mountain mahogany, another hardy resident—all gaunt and spiny and staking out its ground on this high and windy slope.

Who else lived here? Some fur-filled scat told me that coyote had been around—maybe stalking the gophers whose winter tunnels left bulging lines of soil where the ground wasn't as rocky. Chickadee was singing its name. I watched a marsh hawk swoop down on a gray jay that was squawking in protest—usually it was the jays that were doing the pestering. There were still a few bumblebees riding the wind from purple thistle to purple thistle. But it wasn't till I was approaching the aspens that I caught a whiff of another big mammal.

I was just starting in on that final ridge walk. I could see the aspens and Douglas fir on the north slope of the ridge ahead. A thousand feet above me, mountaintop TV towers had just come into view. In the stillness I could hear the warning beeps of a dozer or a backhoe that was moving some dirt around on the transmitter access road, which contoured up the other side of the mountain and ran along the top of the ridge. The air was heavy with elk musk. Tracks and scat were all over the place. I could see where they had flattened the grass, having bedded down here recently. Still, when I heard that first high shriek above me, I thought I was hearing some sort of amplified electronic feedback from the TV tower complex.

Many times, I had heard the bugle of a bull elk off in the distance—one of the great minor keys that graced wild places. But the bugling I heard now was only a few feet above me in a stand of aspens. Like the high notes surging out of John Coltrane's saxophone, this bugle entered my auditory canals, ran right out to the ends of every nerve, and settled in at the base of the spine. I couldn't help but smile.

I followed the ridge up into the aspens. The musk in the air grew thicker. Cool air rising up from a few patches of snow on a north-facing slope mixed in a whiff of pine. I was expecting to see elk. Still, the snap of a broken branch startled me. I heard him crashing through deadfall before I looked down slope and saw that a big bull had stopped and turned to face the danger.

I wasn't feeling especially dangerous—fact is, I was momentarily stunned . . . the proverbial deer in the headlights—looking right into this bull's eyes, and he, less than twenty feet way, looking right back at me. Strips of velvet (a temporary layer of skin on the antler, shed during the rut) dangled from either side of his rack. The rack itself was huge—eight spikes on each antler—big as a rooftop antenna it seemed. As I watched him angling down through the aspens, I could hear the rest of the herd a little further down the hill. Cows squealed at calves and calves bleated back. Another bull bugled nearby. Amidst all the commotion, I heard the high and steady beep of heavy equipment atop the mountain.

Stopping short of an intended ramble up to the ridge where Muir had been, I knew that the action wasn't above timberline, it was down in the trees. If joy was a sign of grace, as I believed it was, then this was a grace-filled encounter—one I savored as I contoured down and around the elk herd. By the time I left the aspens, dropping down into another patch of burnt oak, the herd had settled down—only the occasional bleat or bugle.

Swinging from charred branch to charred branch, I followed a steep draw that led me down into a rocky wash. I followed it out to the edge of the mountain and turned down a two track that ran through the sage, much to the relief of knees and toes and balls of feet. A half mile short of an abandoned homestead, a coyote crossed my path and took off up slope, running a few steps and turning back for a look, again and again, much as I would do inwardly, as I replayed that scene with the bull and the herd, and followed the road down valley.

THAT NIGHT, I PITCHED CAMP IN A LITTLE MEADOW ALONG THE shores of Rush Lake—about a half dozen miles south of Tooelle, and about halfway down the range toward the site of the chemical weapons incinerator. With the old Coleman humming beneath a pot of chicken soup, I took a cold Tecate out of the cooler, settled into a sand chair, and watched the alpenglow slip up and out of high ridge snowfields along the Oquirrh's western slope. I watched distant headlights zig and zag on a switchbacked road that came down off the mountain. House and street lamps shed their glow over the little town of Stockton a few miles to the northeast. Dinner pot steam rose up from the Coleman's blue flame.

I cracked another Tecate, and settled back into my chair to savor a little out-of-the-soup-can cuisine, accompanied with a dipping tortilla or two. Traffic headed both ways on 36, which was a mile or two beyond the far side of the lake, seemed unusually heavy. Maybe this was the changing of the guard at the incinerator, only a dozen miles or so off to southeast. A freight train rumbled down the tracks between the lake and the highway headed, I imagined, in the same direction. As the last of the train cars trailed off into the night, I savored an interlude of quiet.

A while later, I heard wings a flutter and a long skid of a splash as the first of what must have been thirty or forty big birds came in for a landing nearby. Ducks? Geese? In the dark, I couldn't tell. I saw only the dimmest of shadows over near the far shore of the lake. But I would hear them throughout the night: periodic thrashings of wings on water eventually receding into silence. Now and then another train would pass and the entire flock, it seemed, would flap up and off the lake. Later on, one and then another would return. In and out of sleep, I listened as they surfed the dark water and settled into their floating vigil across a rippling Milky Way.

Morning light revealed them to be a flock of white pelicans. Over coffee, I watched them bunch up and thrash the water, herding some hapless carp into the shallows where they became easy prey. After such a feast, it was a marvel they were able to take off at all, but they did, a few at a time, their long wings carrying them north toward the Lake. I would think of them again, driving south on 36, when I heard the official Air Force explanation for the recent crash of an F-16. Apparently, the pilot had been able to parachute to safety but the plane had gone down near the Great Salt Lake. The cause of the crash was a collision with a white pelican.

NEARING THE SOUTHERN TIP OF THE OQUIRRHS, I TURNED ONTO highway 73, drawing ever closer to the incinerator, otherwise known as the Deseret Chemical Disposal Facility. Somewhere off to the south were the earth covered concrete igloos that contained forty percent of the nation's chemical weapons stockpile. The stockpile included mustard gas as well as nerve agent, a volatile chemical related to pesticides like parathion. The most dangerous munitions in storage were M-55 rockets that carried nerve gas in the warhead and explosive propellants in the rear. The most difficult task at the incinerator, one performed with robots, involved separating the nerve gas and the propellant in aging rockets.

In 1994, Steve Jones, a safety inspector whose work had earned him a stellar reputation with the military, cited thousands of safety violations in the design and proposed operation of the incinerator. One hundred and fifty of those violations were categorized as potentially catastrophic. But the higher-ups at EG&G, the defense contractor partnering with the army on this project, downplayed his report, considered him an alarmist, and gave Steve Jones his pink slip.

Two years later, in August of 1996, fewer than seventy-two hours after the incinerator started burning live agent, a leak was detected and the operation shut down. During the first year and a half of the incinerator's operation, alarms designed to detect the release of agent through the incinerator stacks were set off numerous times. In March of 1998, temperatures in the incinerator reached the danger zone when a bomb believed to have been emptied of nerve agent went into the metal parts furnace. The bomb apparently still contained some seventy-five pounds of agent. No one knows for sure if the agent was fully incinerated as the army would like to think, or if it went up the stack. The monitoring system had been temporarily turned off.

I thought about driving down to the Deseret entrance.

A year earlier I'd been out there to the checkpoint. I'd seen the big display sign that touted the number of man hours worked without accident or injury, intended to reassure the public. In light of all the evidence suggesting that military and corporate partners on this project had failed to acknowledge design flaws, safety violations, and mishaps in the incineration process, that big number meant next to nothing. The mission to decommission the chemical weapons stockpile was a worthy and necessary project. The way that it was being done was troubling.

Even more troubling from my vantage point, as I turned away from the incinerator and took the road up Ophir Canyon, was the production of all those chemical weapons in the first place . . . all in the name of security. The question was: whose security? Were the residents of the West Desert and the Wasatch Front any safer? What about workers exposed to the release of agent at Deseret? Granted, these weapons were older, having been produced during the Cold War era. But the "security" rationale that produced them was alive and well and intent on adding to the world's largest stockpile of weapons. When those weapons were obsolete, they too would be shipped off to an out-of-sight, out-of-mind repository like this one. If all went as planned, the "neighbors" would be too few and too poor to put up much resistance.

The production and potential use of chemical, and more recently, nuclear weapons, was based on a world view that either ignored or rejected the ecological reality that everyone lives downstream and downwind from one hazard or another. Fallout from these weapons would not stop at an international border any more than it had stopped at the state line between Nevada and Utah back in the early nuclear testing days. The same held true for the release of nerve agent. While potentially more catastrophic within forty miles or so of the incinerator, wind, water, and the food chain were more than capable of delivering toxins elsewhere. The salt works along the shore of the Great Salt Lake were another convenient means of supplementing that distribution.

As John Muir put it, "when we first try to pick up anything by itself . . . we find it hitched to everything else in the universe." That simple understanding seemed to elude the military, as well as lots of "not-in-my-backyard" folks who figured that Utah or Nevada or any number of western states, had plenty of space for the storage of dangerous waste produced in the name of "homeland security."

The West Desert offered the military and their corporate partners a big back yard for activities that any of the more heavily populated regions of the country would have rejected in a heartbeat. That, in combination with the desire for jobs at any cost in marginal economies, a profound aversion of government regulation (especially those intended to protect soil, air, water, and other species), and the kind of conservativism that equated patriotism with an unconditional support of the military (now an ideological phenomenon that seemed to span all but the most marginalized habitats in America's political ecology), left westerners especially vulnerable to the fallout from a questionable approach to peace and security.

As I drove into the mouth of Ophir Canyon, I understood first hand the out of sight, out of mind syndrome. I was drawn into the immediate scene: a surprisingly lush canyon bottom, at least by Oquirrh standards, lined with willows and cottonwoods. I passed a tidy ranch house next to an irrigated pasture. The same southwest orientation that left the locals especially vulnerable to any mishap at Deseret, seemed to have gathered a little more moisture from the prevailing air stream than other canyons on the southern end of the range. "No camping" signs along the creek told me I wasn't the first to be seduced by this little gem of a canyon.

I drove past several of a dozen cabins and homes that made up the town of Ophir. I passed Minnie's Store on one side of the street and what appeared to be a backyard shrine full of artifacts from the area's mining past on the other. Minnie's was closed. The streets were empty. The only sign of life was a Hereford headed down the road toward me. Further along, under a canopy of cottonwoods and box elders arching over the road—an unusually verdant oasis in these dry and scrubby mountains—I met up with the rest of the herd.

Blocking the road was a mama cow, whose calf was on the opposite side of a cattle guard. In the midst of great bellowing on both sides, it seemed as though one or the other was about to make a leap for it. Then a truck came barreling down the canyon and skidded to a stop. A wrangler jumped out, unlocked and opened an adjacent gate, and afforded the two a reunion.

"Cow's got loose this morning, " he said, a little out of breath. "What a mess. Ya seen any further down the road?"

"Just one," I said, and he vanished as quickly as he had appeared, his truck kicking up dust as he headed into "town."

I continued in the opposite direction, weaving through the rest of the herd, driving a road that crossed the creek several times as I followed it up the canyon. Here and there, parked in camps off to the side of the road, beneath groves of cottonwood, were bunches of trailers, trucks, and campfire rings. It was hunting season. But the hunters were nowhere to be seen. Hoping to get up above all the activity, I drove out to the end of the road, crossed over a creek, and lit out for the timberline.

I followed a trail that snaked up along the creek,splashing through the shallows every couple hundred feet, passing a seep that trickled down over a nearby hillside of mossy rocks. Up the creek another few hundred feet, I paused at the edge of an aspen grove. Crickets, flying grasshoppers, and the breeze rustling through the aspen leaves filled in momentarily for the absence of running water. I looked down through the willows onto a dried creek bed. Backtracking, I found the lower end of a sink where the creek emerged from an underground channel it had taken through the limestone. Out of a pool in the cobbles came the first sign of a stream.

Just as water evokes a sense of hope and promise in dry country, its absence, on some level of one's awareness, can be cause for a little uneasiness. Or so it seemed to me as the sound of the stream grew faint. Back into the trees, my attention was diverted by an inscription carved into a trailside aspen: "Bruce Winston, Clint Mckinney, Bill Olsen, Bruce Elton, 1988—bow hunting— three bucks so far." Must have been a break in the action. No such leisure for a sharp-shinned hawk that came wheeling down through the treetops, ready to pick off any inattentive chipmunks.

Dying time, during these last days of September, was as close as the aspen leaves that littered the trail. Soon the chill would follow the snowline down. So far, only the highest of the peaks and ridges had been dusted with snow. I followed the trail as it contoured around the basin, leading me toward a snow-streaked saddle a mile distant and several hundred feet higher. At intervals along the ridge, red-tailed hawks were riding the thermals. Beyond them, a low-flying 747 disappeared behind the ridge, heading in for a landing at the Salt Lake airport.

Across the upland folds of this basin—stretching out the steps down slope into the aspens, and riding the momentum up again into auburn meadows—I was hitting my stride. Great draughts of good air fueled that sense of body and terrain being in sync—something that happened most readily for me on steady, rolling, or slightly down hill trails. Steps unfurled, as did thoughts, without concern over obstacles or direction. Energy seemed to come on its own accord. The way lay ahead and it was just a matter of aiming oneself in the right direction.

Hitting a stride, like settling or "centering down" into meeting for worship, seemed to open the way for words or phrases to rise up from the depths, in much the same way that the stream emerged from that limestone sink down canyon. In Quaker meeting, the relevance of a word or an image rising in the stillness wasn't always obvious. Often it took further reflection, sometimes prayer, to draw out the truth of any gleanings in the silence. Hitting a stride wasn't meeting for worship, which at its very core, was a community experience. Still, there was some similarity in the quality of the stillness that often accompanied a walk like this. I needed to spend more time with a phrase that had come to mind as I rode the folds of the mountain up toward the ridge. I whispered it . . . "blessed are the peacemakers" . . . and walked with it, and let it settle into breath and step and lay of land.

Up on the saddle, I hit snow. I followed it up the crest of a ridge—the meeting place of the Douglas Fir that grew on the shadier northwest slopes and the last of the aspens reaching up the sunnier southwestern exposure from which I had come. Snowmelt murmured down through the firs. Beads of water shimmered on the aspen leaves that lay in the snow. The breeze picked up as I left the last of the trees behind and walked the final pitch onto a grassy knoll of a summit.

Working as a ranger up in the High Uintas, I had taken to pausing for a moment of two of prayer whenever I reached a summit. It was a good time for a word of thanks—for a mountain, for loved ones, for life. Those thanksgivings in turn reminded me, if only for an instant, of the power and the glory and the source of it all, the one for whom that word of thanks was meant.

Being on a summit, without much shelter from wind, sun or storm, you couldn't help but feel exposed and wary of any menacing clouds out on the horizon. It was an opportunity to experience one's own insignificance and frailty in the presence of a vast and awesome power. Paradoxically, that willingness to be exposed was at the heart of the reorientation and renewal that seemed to follow. It shook the soul and let the glory out.

On this knoll of a summit, looking out past the incinerator and into the West Desert, I wasn't led to give thanks or to settle into a period of silent listening. The only prayer that seemed appropriate was one of petition: for the safe demolition of all the weapons stored on army lands I could see off in the distance, for those who worked out on the base and for others living nearby, for those voices willing to challenge the military, for corporate and military overseers and their awesome responsibility.

A caucus of crows came drifting up the ridge. "Yeah, Yeah, Yeah," they might as well have been saying. "What good are your prayers?"

Hmmn. Well, there were two things I knew for sure. One was that prayer opened, humbled, and "tendered" me. The other was that nothing lived in isolation. If we were all downstream and downwind of one another; if what happened with the air and water in Tooele County would have ripple effects elsewhere, wasn't it consistent to assume the same of soul and spirit? A prayer of petition, it seemed to me was an expression of relationship, if not solidarity. To think like a mountain, as Aldo Leopold once put it, was to understand the world through the lens of interrelationship. It was to hear and value a wolf's howl, not just through the filter of one's own senses, but also from the perspective of the mountain as a whole. This required something like empathy—the ability to imagine from a perspective different than one's own.

Even then, there was a certain wildness in that song we would never fully grasp. All we knew for sure was that it sent a shiver down the spine. It seemed to me that prayer was that way too. My heart was somehow changed. And in that grand old web of interrelationship, maybe others were as well, though there was no way of knowing. Like an inexplicable clacking sound made by white pelicans when the conditions for soaring were especially good, prayer was a song we would never fully understand. In that sense, it too was wild.

LATE THAT NIGHT, I HEARD GUNSHOTS. I HADN'T PLANNED ON SLEEPing out near the incinerator; it just worked out that way. I'd been up several canyons to the east of Ophir, hunting for a place to spend the night without much success.

Up one canyon, dirt bikers were ripping through a big tailings pile. Up another, I ran into fences and no trespassing signs. So I went south into the desert, following the old Pony Express

Route through BLM lands, out toward a little town called Faust. Whether or not the name was related to the legendary magician who sold his soul to the devil, I wasn't sure. But it had some resonance out there on that alkalized plot of desert hardpan, a half-dozen miles or so from the incinerator as the crow flies, where I laid out my tarp and fired up the old Coleman.

In between the yucca and greasewood, I unfolded my chair and settled back to take in the afterglow. As the last light left the Oquirrhs not so very far from the ridge I'd been walking, a wisp of cloud flared up fiery orange, then pink, then red in the distant sky out over Dugway Proving Ground, now home to military experiments with lethal chemicals such as anthrax, ostensibly so they would be able to defend the homeland against attack. One could only hope that the people in charge would be more careful with these chemicals than those who came before them had been with airborne munitions, some of which had come to rest, off target and unexploded, on public lands that surrounded this military reserve. With the Oquirrhs slipping into shadow and the lights of the incinerator flickering out there across the flats, my neighbors at Deseret seemed even closer.

Later, I laid out my bag and slipped into a little mummified sky watching. In and out of sleep, I was keeping track of Aquila, an eagle of stars that traveled east to west across the sky. By that reckoning, it must have been halfway through the night when I heard the first shot. I rolled over and looked out to the east. A mile or two down the road, I saw headlights. A movable spotlight mounted on the cab of a pick-up sent a path of light out through the rabbit brush. I heard another shot. I saw a guy move through the light. Then the truck drove a few hundred feet closer and the routine began all over again.

I had no immediate worries. He was a ways off and he was shooting in the other direction. Surely he would see a white truck before he opened fire out my way. Still, someone out shooting an hour or so after last call might not have the best judgment. I wanted to let him know I was out there. If he thought he'd run into "the law," all the better. So I went over to the truck, waited for an opportune moment when I knew he was situated in his vehicle, and flipped on my headlights, sending the old high beam out across the desert.

After a brief pause, I heard his engine rev and then I watched as he drove by with the hammer down, headed west to Faust. I had nothing against hunting if it was done with humility and reverence. My guess was that the guy down the road had taken a more reckless approach. If he hadn't been poaching, he'd surely been shooting illegally. Though I had never done any hunting myself, I was glad to oblige friends and relatives any time they had venison or elk meat to give away. From the mountain's perspective, as Aldo Leopold pointed out, humans, along with other predators, had a role to play in periodically thinning wild game populations. The alternative—diseased and starving wildlife populations—was not a pretty picture. But reckless killing was another thing altogether. Leopold had seen the "green fire dying" in the eyes of a wolf unnecessarily shot. What "fires" had just gone out in the rabbit brush down the road?

No telling. And there was no getting back to sleep. It was a little after three. The monks at the Abbey of the Holy Trinity, a few hours up the road in Huntsville, would soon be gathering for vigil—the first "office" or community worship of the day. Like that guy headed west to Faust, I liked an empty road at night, though for different reasons. Like the monks up in Huntsville, I was drawn to the quiet expectancy of pre-dawn prayer time, known in monastic tradition as the nightwatch. So I loaded up the truck, and turned out onto the road toward the little town of Fairfield, figuring I'd ride this nightwatch out on the road.

Well before the rising hum of traffic would begin, this would be a good time of day to re-enter the urban corridor that ran along the Wasatch Front from Provo through Salt Lake and on up toward Ogden. The plan was to round the bend out by Point of the Mountain. From there I'd head northwest to the Butterfield Canyon Road, which bisected the Oquirrhs roughly in half. I'd driven across the range a time or two, but I'd never lingered up top and it seemed as though it would be a good perch for the sunrise.

Out on the road, my headlights occasionally caught the eyes of critters looking back my way—jackrabbits, mostly, a couple of small owls out chasing voles and mice. Coyotes were probably on the prowl as well, though I didn't see any. As the lights of Deseret fell back behind me, I drove north and east through sage and rabbit brush toward the shadowy hulk of the Oquirrhs. My thoughts returned to the words I had been walking with at the head of Ophir Canyon.

"Blessed are the Peacemakers." This simple declaration, spoken by Jesus in his sermon on the mount, was one of eight "beatitudes" or blessings that gave his followers a guide to live by. Blessed also were: the poor in spirit, those who mourned, the meek, the merciful, the pure in heart, those who were hungry and thirsty for righteousness, and those who were persecuted for righteousness' sake. All would be comforted, all would be blessed, all would be filled with God's presence, Jesus said.

The crowds that gathered to hear Jesus, Matthew says, were "astounded at his teaching, for he taught them as one having authority, and not as their scribes." He wasn't from Jerusalem, the center of religious thought and tradition; he was from Nazareth. His authority came not from the temple but from the desert, where his soul had been opened and emptied; from the streets where he had established himself as a healer; from the mountain where those who heard him knew his teachings were for real. As a teacher coming from the wild edge of the religious culture of the time, he was alive and vibrant and beyond the control of the powers and principalities. It was no coincidence that he taught the beatitudes on a mountain; in the Jewish tradition, the mountain was associated with the authority of prophets like Moses and Elijah, and with the Presence of God they encountered there. In God's wildness, Jesus offered hope.

Reflecting on all of this, I was getting a little wild myself. Pedal close to metal, I was hitting around eighty on the old speedometer as I approached the town of Fairfield. Whoa. No sign of any flashing lights . . . seems I'd managed to coast through town unnoticed. It was a good thing that John Muir never got behind the wheel. I imagined him driving into town from the Oquirrhs, steering wheel in one hand, a bunch of mountain lilies clutched in the other, showering his specimens with holy praise. Even Muir had to settle down a little when he came back into town.

Soon I was driving into a neighborhood on the southern edge of the Salt Lake Valley. I stopped for coffee at a Maverick that had just opened its doors, tuned into a late night blues show on KRCL, and drove with Lightning Hopkins through the suburban hinterlands of Bluffdale and Riverton. In a culture bent on optimism at all costs, the Blues were a corrective voice. While culture said avoid grief and despair at all costs, lest you be regarded as depressed, depressing, or deranged, the Blues said: "Go ahead . . . you gotta feel it to heal it." If the Oquirrhs had a song, it was a song with plenty of blue notes. Blessed, the beatitudes told me, were those who heard them.

B.B. King made his blue notes heard, as I broke out of the suburban scene. After many a sleeping-neighborhood meander, I drove onto a road that skirted the eastern flank of the Oquirrhs. Soon I was turning into the mouth of Butterfield Canyon, heading up the switchbacks toward the divide between the eastern and western slopes. A mountain road like this, it seemed to me, was a good one for the nightwatch. Time and again in the gospels, Jesus had gone up a mountain at night to pray. Time and again he had come down the mountain empowered.

It was still plenty dark up the canyon. I drove the switchbacks nice and slow, watching for deer as I came up through the oaks. I thought I had once seen a steep road heading north and west along the ridge on the backside of the pass. I came around the last of the switchback curves and there it was. I took it, not knowing where it would lead me, except that it promised more altitude.

Heading west, I could see the lights of Tooele and the army depot a ways off into the night. Whoever the peacemakers were in our time, they had nothing to do with the "peacekeeper" missiles of Desert Storm fame. Protecting "national interests" was about control, not peacemaking. It was about maintaining the three p's: power, prestige, and possessions; (four p's if you count petroleum). Jesus' peace, a peace that came only after a long time of trial in the desert, had nothing to do with protecting self-interests. It had everything to do with letting them go. The prayer that Jesus taught on the mountain made that very clear. As I'd once heard Franciscan priest Richard Rohr put it, "we can't say 'thy kingdom come,' unless we're also willing to say, 'my kingdom go.'" To believe that, and to attempt to live into it, was to walk out on the wild side.

In the early morning hours, the western slope of the Oquirrhs, shielded as it was from city lights, felt like the wilder side of the range. A switchback curled back on itself like a loop in a slack rope. I nudged the truck into the pullout on the brink of a precipice, the only place to park. A mile or so below was Salt Lake City in all its neon glory. And I invoked a traditional prayer for the celestial oversight of parking brakes.

There was a hint of light in the sky above the jagged outline of the Wasatch, but it was only a hint. I started walking up the road, thinking about the night stalkers who were still out and about. Plenty of cougar followed the deer herds through this Oquirrh Mountain scrub. I was wary, taking comfort in the margins of open ground between my path down the middle of the road, and the edge of the oaks off to either side of me. Nothing like thoughts of a predator to keep one awake and watchful.

As soon as there was enough light, I left the road and took off up a steep, sage-covered slope. Passing through a stand of stunted aspen, something spooked. A buck and two does rose up from the sage less than fifty feet away. The buck gave a snort as they loped off down the eastern side of the ridge—shadowy in the gloaming, then hidden in the scrub.

A few more zigs and zags and the terrain leveled out. Below me was an inviting saddle; beyond that the crest of a hill not unlike the one I was standing on. Similar waves and troughs lay further along the ridge, all the way up to the blinking lights of the TV transmission tower on a summit to the north.

Heading down the saddle and up the other side, I might have guessed that I was closing in on Kennecott property. Still, as I topped out on the second wave, the steady drone of heavy equipment took me by surprise, as did the big hole itself. Along the rim of the hole below me, were metal storage buildings and beehive shaped piles of waste rock, neatly arranged. On the far side, a band of aspens came down to the edge where the mountain left off and the pit began. In between, one truck geared down as it began the descent, while another rumbled out of the pit with another load of the mountain. This place never slept.

Below and off to my west, an orange-capped hunter drove out to the edge of a turnaround overlooking the pit. He rolled down his window and scanned the hill, gradually raising his gaze up to the crest on which I was perched. I waved. He waved back. Then he rolled up his window and drove back down the same ridge road on which I had parked a mile or two back.

In the interval between first light and sun up, the mountain came alive with hunters. Another truck pulled up below me and several guys staked out their ground on the saddle between my perch and the previous hilltop. They were scanning the scrub oak along the eastern slope for movement, but the deer had already come around to the north face of the hill. I could hear them breaking through crusted snow in between the Douglas Firs shading the slope below me. They were headed down toward the pit which, as private land, was safe refuge . . . at least from the guys in orange.

What instincts were guiding them toward safety? If there was wisdom in their wildness, what might we find in our own wild hearts? It had been one hundred and thirty years since John Muir had pondered that question: "If a magnetic needle, a strip of particle of iron be shown its way, shall the soul . . . be left unguided?" In another notebook, he answered his own question: "We are governed more than we know, and most when we are wildest."

Part Three: Home Ground

On the Hermit's Trail

IF A RAVEN LEFT A PERCH NEAR OUR HOME IN CRESTONE, COLORADO, flew several miles to the east and one mile up to the fourteen thousand foot spine of the Sangre de Cristo Range; if it continued south over the Crestone Needle, Mt. Blanca, Culebra Peak, and eventually down into New Mexico; if it flew further south, over the cirques of Wheeler Peak, New Mexico's highest mountain, south over Taos Pueblo, farther south over the rolling ponderosa forests of the Pecos Wilderness; if it veered ever so slightly to the east, toward the meeting place of the Great Plains and the southern end of the Sangres, it might just come to rest on the high point of two turtle-shaped granite massifs. This would be the summit of Hermit's Peak.

From here, the lights of Las Vegas, New Mexico shimmer off to the south at night and the sun comes up somewhere over Texas. From here, you can look up north toward the towns of Watrous and Wagon Mound, where the old trade and travel route known as the Santa Fe Trail took a turn out onto the Great Plains. From here, a steep and winding trail leads down to a shallow cave where the hermit—for whom this peak was named—once lived.

I first noticed Hermit's Peak in August of 1999. Grace and I had just left Santa Fe where we had been visiting with Father Anderson Bakewell, our friend, my mentor, and the only relative I knew of who had ever set foot in a seminary (which was where I was headed for one last year of study). Before we left, the Padre had given his blessing to our baby-to-be—a baby who, he reminded us, would grow up to be a lover of adventure. "It's in the genes," he said.

Knowing the Padre had cancer and knowing we wouldn't be back for another year or so, our visit was bittersweet. I held on to the image of his smile and his wave as we drove along the southernmost edge of the Sangre de Cristos. Following the long bend of the highway headed into Las Vegas, New Mexico, on the first leg of our road trip east following the Santa Fe Trail, periodically scanning the rolling Ponderosa foothills off to the north, I couldn't help but notice some stunning granite cliffs that rose into a flat-topped summit on the horizon.

Over a bowl of green chili in Las Vegas, I checked the road atlas. It must have been Hermit's Peak I'd just seen—wonder who the hermit was? A quick look through a Santa Fe Trail guide by historian Marc Simmons, told me the following:

> The peak is named in honor of Giovanni Maria Augustini. He arrived in Las Vegas in 1863 with a freight caravan of the Romero's . . . one of two leading merchant families in town. Augustini reportedly performed a number of cures and miracles, but the crowds he attracted caused him to flee to the flat-topped mountain 14 miles east of Las Vegas and resume his life as a hermit.

FOR A SEMINARIAN INTERESTED IN BOTH MOUNTAINS AND PRAYER, this was tantalizing stuff. As we drove further east, and as I was able to glean more information from various sources along the way, I told Grace the hermit's story.

In 1863, at the age of sixty-two, Giovanni Augustini approached Don Miguel Romero, a trader who was headed west out of Council Grove, Kansas, bound for Las Vegas, New Mexico. Augustini asked if he could join Romero's' caravan and offered a letter of introduction which had been signed by the commander of the American garrison in Council Grove:

> "To whom it may concern: This paper certifies that the bearer, Giovanni Augustini, is a missionary who has lived in the area for about forty-five days. He has been in the St. Louis district for several years where he has lived in caves, dugouts, and in the open, subsisting only on vegetables and corn meal mush. He has befriended the poor and helped the ill. He meditates constantly; indeed he must be a holy man."

Though he gratefully accepted Don Romero's invitation to come along, Augustini politely declined invitations to ride in the caravan wagons, choosing instead to walk all 550 miles to Las Vegas. He spent his nights out past the edge of camp, where some say he passed the time plucking out hymns and other tunes on an old mandolin.

El Hermitano, as he came to be known in Las Vegas, had come from a well-to-do family in Italy. He enjoyed the benefits of a good education, which may have included training for the priesthood. Eventually, he felt called to lead a solitary life. Why he was drawn to the hermit's way was not clear, although there were rumors of disputes with family and/or church authorities, not to mention another lingering story about a love affair gone bad. In any event, he lived the life of a wandering ascetic for thirty-five years, holing up in caves mostly, many of them out past the edge of small mountain villages first in France and Spain, then in South America, then Mexico, then Cuba, then Canada, and then finally in the United States. Occasionally, he would come into nearby towns to visit friends maybe take communion at a Catholic church. Sometimes he traded carvings and handmade trinkets for groceries—mostly corn meal.

What happened to the hermit in Las Vegas may have typified his experiences elsewhere. For a while he made himself at home in a cave tucked away in a canyon on Don Miguel Romero's ranch. But over time, his occasional appearances in Las Vegas, his willingness to receive visitors and offer them counsel, and his abilities as an herbalist who would accompany his treatments with a prayer or two, added to his legendary status as a healer and a holy man. Locals would pitch their tents out near Augustini's cave just to be in the presence of "El Santo Hermitano."

So much for solitude. Increasing numbers of visitors forced Augustini to move once again, this time to the big mountain he had admired from the Santa Fe Trail, which he could now see off to the north and west from the Romero Ranch, its two great cliffs cresting like giant waves of stone. On the mountain's flat-topped ridge he would find a spring, along with grassy clearings surrounded by aspen, pine, spruce, and fir. And he would choose a shallow cave, just below the 10,260 foot summit, for his shelter. For four years or so, this would be the hermit's home.

As we drove further east onto the Great Plains, following the Cimarron route of the Santa Fe Trail, I imagined the hermit walking an especially thirsty fifty-mile stretch known as the *jornada*, where water holes were scarce, if they existed at all. I thought of him playing his mandolin the night we camped along a river bottom in the Oklahoma panhandle and followed a set of Sante Fe Trail wagon ruts—probably 150 years old—out into the prairie grass at dusk. I thought of him again as we drove east past Pawnee Rock under the glare of a high noon sun, one of the only breaks in the flatland monotony that he would have known all too well on his long trek west to Las Vegas.

Further into Kansas, we rode the oceanic swells of the Flint Hills, stopping for eggs and biscuits at a place called The Hayes House (founded in 1857 and open for business ever since) in Council Grove. Afterward, we tried to walk off a biscuit or two, following the self-guided tour we'd found in an historical brochure that led us to another one of the hermit's cave dwellings, this one on a hill on the edge of downtown Council Grove. If his letter of introduction were any indication, he would have been well-regarded in town. And it seemed unlikely that this small cave in the side of a hill, so very close to Main Street, would have offered much solitude. Maybe that's why he had been anxious to move on.

But even in a cave as remote as the one he would later find on Hermit Peak, Augustini was unable to live the solitary life he sought. Ironically, he seemed to have a penchant for winning friends and admirers who would later rob him of his solitude. After four years on Hermit Peak, he lit out for new territory once again. This time he chose to make his home in a roomy and dry-bottomed cave in a foothill oasis on the flanks of the Organ Mountains near Las Cruces, New Mexico. As he had on Hermit's Peak, he lit a bonfire periodically to assure a friend living in the nearby valley he was all right. Toward the end of April 1869, when Colonel Albert Fountain did not see the hermit's fire at the appointed time, he organized a posse and they rode up to the cave. There they found Augustini lying face down on a crucifix with a dagger in his back.

Why would anyone want to murder such a person? Some say that roving Apaches or maybe an outlaw on the move killed the hermit, but it's hard to imagine what anyone would have gained in murdering this humble wanderer. He had no possessions other than his clothes, an old mandolin, a Bible, and maybe a few other religious books. Was his murder an inside job? It wouldn't have been the first time church authorities perceived an outrider mystic as a threat.

More that a century has passed since the hermit's death, which still remains a mystery, as does much of his life. What called Augustini to become a solitary? Was it a movement away from something or an attraction to some other way of knowing this life? What unmet longings kept him moving from place to place?

In South America and perhaps elsewhere, Catholic bishops had invited him to take on a parish. But it was not his way. He remained true to his calling as a solitary. The stories and legends that lingered along his path were unanimous in their description of a kind, humble, and devout wanderer, with a special gift for healing.

The edge wasn't just an escape for him; it was a place from which to engage the world. The same is true for many Quakers. The contemplative side of Quakerism—the attraction to silence, to stillness, to emptying, and thereby to opening, makes it possible for me to think of myself as part of a long line of seekers whose experiences of divinity tended to be more abstract and less easily named. We Quakers have our metaphors—the Inward Teacher, the Inner Light—but you can't help but travel gently with words, when silence is understood as the best way forward in discerning any truth.

Yet Quaker worship is also about living and speaking out of that relationship with truth—an orientation which very often challenges the status quo. Voices I have found in the Quaker tradition help me to understand the roles and responsibilities of someone drawn to a life on the "edge of the village."

The hermit's example, extreme as it may have been in his devotion to a deeply solitary and prayer-centered way of life, would strike many nowadays as absurd, if not deranged. (Then again many hermits might say the same of the culture from which they have chosen to live apart.) But even in his eccentricity, even in his own peculiar and radical detachment, Giovanni Augustini managed to engage those he met in meaningful ways. And his intent may not have been as odd as one might think.

Anyone on the trail of the Spirit might do well to ask the kinds of questions El Hermitano likely pondered: What matters? On what ground will I choose to build a life? How do I know what is real and what is illusory? Who/how am I supposed to be?

SEVERAL YEARS AFTER THAT GREAT PLAINS CROSSING WHEN I FIRST learned about the Hermit, I am driving west out of Crestone, Colorado. It is an hour before dawn on a cold November morning. The brightest light on the edge of town is a marquee in front of the Baptist church—black letters on a backdrop shining blue and red which says: "A dead end is a good place to turn around." Ironically, the town of Crestone, including this church, and the adjacent Baca Grande settlement where I live, are about as close to being at the end of the road as a place can get in the lower forty-eight.

I am riding with my friend Will Miles, a retired psychology professor from the University of Alaska, who has recently moved here from his home near Wasilla. Neither of us turned around at this particular end of the road. As Quakers, it might be said that we both followed our respective leadings here. We share a love of mountains on the edge of which we have chosen to make our homes. And we appreciate the quality of silence toward which Quakers are naturally drawn and in which we both feel a little closer to that which we understand as holy.

Early Quakers were referred to as a "peculiar people," because of their plain dress, plain speech, and unusual form of worship. So perhaps it should come as no surprise that Will and I have landed in a community where some of our neighbors might be thought of as peculiar, though, in this case, for different reasons. When the word was out that downtown Crestone was soon to have its first drinking establishment, I had visions of the barroom scene in Star Wars—all sorts of odd characters gathered on the edge of the interstellar frontier for a night on the town before heading off into the great unknown. If you ask around long enough in Crestone, you may find a few people who claim to be from different planets. Others claim to have met alien travelers. I follow the lead of a friend, a long time resident here, who says he puts all of this stuff in his "I don't know file," meaning "well, whatever . . . I just don't know much about such things."

What I do know about this place, and the reason why Grace and I ended up here, is that it is also a tolerant and very contemplative community full of seekers and practitioners of many traditions—some of whom have moved here from other countries. They are living out of stories not often heard on most American main streets. Conversations at the post office are decidedly different.

We came here first, not with the intention of staying, but with the desire to be around a dozen or so Carmelite monks whose writings I had come to be familiar with in their publication *Desert Call*. These Carmelites, self-described as earthy mystics, were also lovers of literature and mountains, not to mention their obvious calling to a life of solitude, silence, and prayer. So we came here wanting to learn, to be a part of the lay community that had grown up around the monastery, and to discern our way forward as a young family intent on embracing the kinds of values that we held in common with them.

After finding out about a place to live for a few months, we turned up at their contemplative mass one day with our daughter Rosalea, who was closing in on her first birthday. She took to the Carmelites immediately and wasn't shy about expressing herself, especially when the priest held up the host for a blessing before serving communion. Her debut at mass might best be described as raucous, leaving us feeling a little sheepish in our first introductions to the monks with whom we'd been corresponding. "We thought Rosalea was a contemplative," Grace explained to our new friends after mass, "but we're starting to think she may be more of a charismatic." Rosalea clearly had the gift for speaking in the kinds of tongues that only babies know and understand.

Though I like long stretches of solitude, I am not a solitary as are many hermits and quasi-hermits in Crestone. Still, radical solitude intrigues me, which is maybe why I am still interested in the hermit and why we are making this trip down to Hermit Peak to try and find his cave, which I have so far—after several trips to the summit—been unable to find. That the hermit was living on the high edge of the same mountain range that has become my home makes the trip even more meaningful. And this time the prospects for finding the cave are good, since we will be climbing with a Forest Service archaeologist who has actually been there, and who has also done plenty of research on the historical value of the place, especially for those in northern New Mexico, where the hermit's story is very much alive.

Will is a particularly good traveling companion on this trip, not only because he's spent a lot of time in the Alaskan backcountry, and not only because he is a genial lover of adventure, but also because he wrote his PhD thesis on the psychology of religious experience. As we are driving south out of Raton, New Mexico, the early morning sun revealing the kind of clear skies that bode well for our climb up Hermit's Peak, I ask him about the psychology of those who are called to be hermits. His answer, measured and well-spoken, suggests a continuum between those whose personalities might be construed as abnormal, and those who are simply listening to their deepest yearnings or what Socrates called their "daemon," which, we decide, might be likened to the Quaker notion of the Inward Teacher, or Christ. The daemon, he explains, is that inward voice or prompting that might lead one to live out a particular calling toward wholeness. How does one know whether it is the "daemon" or some collective of inner demons, that someone like Augustini is listening to? Will responds with the proposition that those hermits listening to the latter, would have little to offer, or for that matter little interest in their fellow human beings. This was hardly the case from what I know of the hermit's story, which suggests to both of us that he may have been well-guided in following his inclination toward the solitary way.

As we begin our climb up Hermit's Peak with archaeologist Jeremy Kulisheck a few hours later, we realize the logistics of living out his particular calling as a mountain hermit, particularly one who would have been in his sixties at the time, had to be daunting. He wouldn't have had the advantage of our winter gear—heavy waterproof boots and gaiters and all the warm clothes we are climbing in, not to mention the snowshoes we will soon strap on to make our way across snowdrifts, which are at least a couple feet deep. Nor would he have had the radio Jeremy is packing in as a precaution. This was a man who likely slept in the same overcoat that he wore most every day. His only hiking aid was a long staff with a bell on the end of it, announcing his arrival when he came down off the mountain to visit friends in nearby villages.

We are nearing the top of a steep set of switchbacks that take us up through a notch between two flat peaks, the higher of which is where the hermit lived. Unlike previous visits here in warmer weather, when the chatter of chickadees and juncos inhabiting the Ponderosa pines was constant, the forest is strangely silent today, except for the wind that breaks over the top of the ridge above us and except for the conversation I have with Jeremy.

It is gratifying to meet someone else who has taken a deep interest in the hermit's story even if we are devoting precious oxygen to our exchange of information. But Jeremy is doing most of the talking since his research on the historical value of this place—which for the most part has to do with the hermit's story and those who continued, long after he was gone, to make pilgrimages to his cave—has been more extensive than my own. And I wonder if there are any remnants of the informal brotherhood of locals, once known as the Sociedad del Hermitano. Initiated by one of Don Manuel Romero's sons in the early twentieth century, I'd read that for many years they had made regular pilgrimages to the hermit's dwelling. Did anyone still do that?

"What I can tell you is that we talked with people in the community for whom this place is still important," he said, "but those interviews are confidential." Fair enough. I am content to know that the hermit's cave is still significant to some, if not revered.

We approach the top of the switchbacks and can see light breaking through the trees ahead. It is well past lunchtime. I tell Jeremy that, in honor of the hermit, we are packing in a pot of cold corn meal mush for lunch. Truth is, as we stake out our perch on the edge of a magnificent ledge overlooking the route that we drove to get to the trailhead—a high mountain valley and the rolling ponderosa forests surrounding it—our provisions are more enticing than the hermit's ascetic cuisine would have been. Will has packed in a loaf of homemade banana bread, most of which we devour, in anticipation of the climb ahead of us.

The wind picks up, there is a squall spitting snow off to the west, and it is getting late—only a couple of hours of light remaining of this short January day. Will nods up toward the snow and points to his watch. We don't want to get stuck up here, much as it might add to our vicarious trip into the hermit's terrain.

So we pack up and carry on, soon venturing into deep drifts, our steps now falling through several feet of snow. I unload my pack and take off the snowshoes that I mistakenly thought, earlier on along the snowless part of this trail, we might not need. As I strap on the Sherpa Claws, the wind blows even harder, the squall appears to be settling in over the mountain, and the sun we enjoyed at lunch is all but gone.

I take the lead as Jeremy brings up the rear. On this ascent, the trail looks different. It is hard to tell where it actually goes. I depend on my memory of this place and the lay of this slope, which we follow up though a widely spaced stand of aspen, hopefully to the hermit's spring. From there I know I can find the way to the summit, following what's left of the stations of the cross that were once kept up by those who came to pay their respects to the hermit and his life of prayer. But I'm still not sure I can find the spring in all this snow. And I am beginning to feel anxious that we are going to run out of daylight, and I can tell by the look in Will's eye that he is nervous, too. It is too cold and too windy to stand still out here on this exposed side of the mountain, and I've got too much adrenalin pumping through my veins. We press on.

I am relieved to break out into a clearing that looks familiar and sure enough, I can see the spring up ahead. I feel a surge of energy and pick up the pace. Will and I wait for Jeremy above a small well where the hermit probably got his water and where those who have since come to pay their respects likely gather theirs. I've heard stories told of those who believe this water has healing powers. I am certainly feeling restored having found the way here again. And when Jeremy arrives and suggests that, with our headlamps, all we'll need to do is get down the switch-backs before dark—he has made the descent that way before—I am less anxious. Besides, the sun has come back out, throwing lovely horizontal shafts of light through the clearings in these trees. Onward.

After a meander up a steadily rising trail through aspen and fir, past the old crosses that reassure us we are nearing the high point, we emerge in a clearing and the trees part to reveal the incredible expanse of the Great Plains rolling off to the east. Will and I walk out the ledge above the big cliff I first saw from the highway. But the wind is so strong we pull back and wait for Jeremy, whom we follow along the edge of the mountain, look-ing for the way down to the cave. It has been a while, Jeremy says, and it all looks so different under the snow. A while later, he tells us we have gone too far and we backtrack. I wonder if he'll be able to find the way. Moments later, I follow him down off the side of the mountain and past a tree upon which some-one has tacked an image of the Virgin of Guadalupe. We are getting close. Now a few twists and turns down a steep slope and we are standing in front of . . . well I would hardly describe it as a cave . . . more like an overhang. Is this it?

"A humble place for a humble man," says Jeremy.

Humble indeed. It is hard to tell, given the rocky and uneven ledges under this overhang, how the hermit would have gotten any rest here. To make matters worse, there appears to be a seep in the rock wall underneath the overhang. Water trickles out and covers the floor of this cave with a sheet of ice. It does seem to be out of the wind, at least if today's wind from the west is the prevailing wind around here. But still. Jeremy points out the remnants of a rock wall, part of a small cabin believed to have been built here by Don Romero's sons to add to the hermit's shelter. He says there is no evidence that there were any Indian inhabitants here prior to the hermit. At best, for them, he says, this would have been an overnight bivouac.

Not for the hermit. If there were a real estate listing for this spot, it would read, "Especially rustic shelter for the backcountry lover . . . views, views, views." The view *is* astounding, nothing but a few firs and then space all the way out to Las Vegas. But a good view won't keep you warm and my respect for the hermit's stalwart resilience soars. This was one formidable solitary. And I can see from the votive candles placed along rock ledges that others have also come here out of great respect, perhaps even regarding his stay on the mountain as inconceivable without a little supernatural support. At the very least, the hermit must have had some serious mojo to pull this off.

But our mojo is fading with the light and we have to move on down the mountain. We hustle down slope to the switchbacks. I enjoy the subtle floating sensation of riding the old sherpa claws across the top layer of these drifts, feeling euphoric about having finally found my grail up here—the elusive cave—and feeling a little more in awe of the man who, for a few years, called it home.

Back down in the trees, all but the last sliver of daylight gone out of the sky, Will and Jeremy strap on their headlamps. Since I forgot mine, I walk between them. The trail ahead is obvious enough in the pools of light, the mood is jovial, and the talk is easy, ranging over all sorts of topics, always returning, after a while, to the hermit. Almost out to the road now, I ask Jeremy what he thinks the hermit's time up here was all about.

"I don't think you can spend time up there on the side of the mountain and not think that he was drawn toward some kind of transcendence." Having just come off the mountain, and knowing what I know about the hermit's life, I believe he is right. Of course the word *transcendence* gets airy in a hurry if you try to pin it down. What is one trying to transcend? And why?

Both Will and I might say we live at the end of road to be closer to the mountains. And that's part of it. But I think it's a yearning more complicated than that. It is the same yearning that attracts us to solitude, though not as radically as the hermit, as well as silence and stillness. To what end? I suspect the hermit would have been more confident in his answer to that question than either Will or I might be.

As I ponder all of this, I stumble over a rock in the trail. I wait for Will and the beam shining off of his headlamp to catch up. As is often the case, what is right for me in this moment—slow down . . . wait for the light . . . try not to get out in front of it— is also, for now anyway, all I really need to know.

The View from Vulture Gulch

HOME. LAND. SECURITY. THESE THREE WORDS EVOKE THE STRONGEST of human yearnings: for home—a shelter, the place that calls us back, the center from which we experience the world; for land—the ground that sustains us; for security—safety, relationships in which we care and are cared for, freedom from high doses of anxiety and danger.

HOME. LAND. SECURITY. IN GENESIS 2, AFTER FORMING "EVERY animal of the field and every bird of the air," the Creator brought them before the first human to see how they might be named. Naming the world, this creation story tells us, was the part of the human vocation that initiated our primeval sense of place.

Out walking with my daughter Rosalea, I give her the names of things—chickadees and prickly pear; juncos and rabbit brush; rosehips and chipping sparrows. Halfway through her second year in this world, she knows gray jay squawk and chickadee serenade. She can tell the difference between the blue grama and the Indian rice grasses that grow out behind our house. She can identify the sprigs of pinyon (*pin-yone*, as she pronounces it) and juniper (*june-ah*-purr) I give her to hold in her hand. She knows the leaves of scrub oaks and aspens. She lights up whenever we walk through patches of the spiky yucca, knowing that their pods—dry, hard, and full of seeds—make wonderful rattles. By the time she is two, she knows more about her place than I knew about my new home in the west after my first year of college. One day, Rosalea and I are following a sandy two track that runs through a stand of Ponderosa pine. Recently, she has managed to link her first few steps and she is now eager to walk on her own. I scan the ground ahead for cactus, yucca, and other possible hazards. Seeing none, I turn her loose. She takes a half dozen steps, bends over, promptly gathers up a handful of dirt and pine needles and stuffs it all in her mouth. Naming one's place is just the beginning.

HOME. LAND. SECURITY. ON THE WAY TO THE NORTH CRESTONE Creek Trailhead, we hear the news on the radio. The World Trade Towers are on fire. The Pentagon has been hit. We walk the trail up past the old gold diggings, past deep eddied pools below big rocks and falling water, through a yellowed grove of aspen only now beginning to let go of those first few leaves. Rosalea rides quietly in the pack, looking over my shoulder at the trail ahead of us. In that moment, I want nothing more for my daughter than this "true blue dream" of mountain sky.

"*Huh-tail, huh-tail,*" she says as we pass a patch of horsetails, a tubular green plant that turns up in low shady spots where moisture gathers.

"Horsetail," I say.

"*Huh-tail,*" she says again. For her, our usual routine hasn't changed. For that I am grateful.

Farther along, Grace and I wonder aloud who was behind the attack and what their motives were. Gradually, our words trail off. We keep on walking, rising up over the creek as we follow the switchbacks, looping back and forth along this south-facing slope. Soon we break through the last of the aspens, walk out onto open ground, and see the big walls of granite to our east. Once known as the spine of the earth to the Jicarilla Apache, it is the Spanish name for this range—Sangre de Cristo—that we have inherited. Blood of Christ. It is a name that has its own resonance on this day of human suffering. And it is a name that always seems right at the end of the day when peaks like the one at the head of this canyon gather in the last light.

What has happened in Manhattan, on the far edge of this big country, seems so far away. But fewer than a hundred miles to our north and east, sequestered inside of the great granitic core of Cheyenne Mountain near Colorado Springs, the heart of North American Air Defense (NORAD), all eyes are scanning the radar screens for anything out of the ordinary. A few hours to our south is Los Alamos and the national lab where the atom bomb was developed, surely one of the military hubs now identified as a vulnerable target.

Down off the mountain later that morning, we drive past a group of college kids in a creek side campground. Some are crying. Some look puzzled, numb, or despondent as they sit on rocks and logs around the van whose radio we hear as we drive by.

Back home, we bring sandwiches out behind the house and settle in beside a big pinyon tree, catching the latest news reports on KRZA, the community radio station for our region and our primary link to the rest of the world. I am grateful that I can't see those horrific images replaying again and again on the television news. That Rosalea is still young enough to be spared our shock and sadness is some consolation.

Then again, we wonder what she has picked up from our eyes, from our voices, and from the words she hears on the radio report. A reporter's voice estimates the death toll. Another commentator thanks him for his on-the-scene report.

"Goodbye, people," Rosalea says, while an ethereal piano plays in between news segments.

"Maybe that's enough for now," Grace says, as she walks over to shut off the radio.

HOME. LAND. SECURITY. DECEMBER. FIRST SNOWS AND FRESH TRACKS. Rosalea peers out over my shoulder, as we follow a rabbit's trail down the Forest Service Road toward town. "Where does the rabbit live?" she asks.

"Rabbits like little holes in the ground," I say. I am reminded of the President's words for the terrorists on the radio earlier that morning: "we're gonna do whatever it takes to find 'em and we're gonna smoke 'em out of their holes." That metaphor doesn't work for me. The phenomenon of terrorism seems more akin to an invasion of thistles, many of which have already gone to seed. You can hack down the thistles all you want, but you only spread the seed and invite more thistles. Let's bring the criminals to justice, sure, but let's also find out how we have given them the grounds on which to thrive and do something about that too.

"Where do the bears live?" Rosalea asks, as we continue down the road toward town. I am glad for the diversion.

"They like dark places," I say. "Sometimes they dig holes. Sometimes they sleep in caves or old mine shafts." I am thinking of previous walks past all the caves, all the old glory holes, and all the bear trees up nearby Burnt Gulch. There I had shown Rosalea all the bear claw markings left behind by younger bears that had climbed up the aspens. "*Ohhhhhh*" she said, running her fingers across the scarred bark.

"Yeeeha," she whoops now, as we come around the bend and town appears, a half-mile or so down the road, nestled in the cottonwoods along Crestone Creek.

"Yeeeha," I answer, as is our custom on this final descent into town. With several hundred residents, the town of Crestone includes the Crestone Mart or C-mart (where you can buy a quart of milk, rent a video, pick up a bag of nails and some two-by fours), the post office (town hub), and 21st Amendment liquor store. There's a motel, a Laundromat, and a small log chapel that is open all the time. At Black Bear Video, you can rent a foreign film. At Curt's store, you can pick up some fresh produce, some locally grown beef, maybe a pint of Ben & Jerry's. Or you can gas up for the occasional run into bigger towns like Alamosa or Salida, both of which are about an hour away.

In a place as remote as Crestone, it is possible to live into an illusion that urban areas or foreign countries have little to do with one's own home, land, or security. Similarly, in this country, bounded as we are on both sides by the great oceans, it is possible for us to imagine we can maintain a level of homeland security beyond the capablity of other countries. America as gated community. But homeland security is only real when it is just as real for Afghanis, Iraqis, Palestinians, Israelis, and the rest of our global neighborhood.

On this morning, we find little traffic downtown—only Dogman dragging a muffler as he drives his station wagon over to his usual parking space across from Curt's store. We leave the pavement, and walk the dirt road down past the cemetery ("Burial Permit Required: Please check in before you check out," the sign says). As usual, Rosalea notices the brightly colored whirligig that someone has planted, in lieu of flowers, next to a headstone. A few coyote yip somewhere out in the edgeland forest, which soon gives way to the cactus, rabbit brush, yucca and grasses that cover the valley floor.

"I want to go hug the coyote," Rosalea says.

"They're a long ways off, honey," I say.

"I want to hug the coyote," she insists.

"Coyotes don't like to be hugged," I allow.

"I want to hug the coyote," she continues, her insistence morphing into the tears that tell me she will soon be nodding off. A few hundred feet down the road, passing through a gate in the fence, and farther out into this high altitude savannah known as the San Luis Valley, Rosalea gives me her mittens, places a thumb in her mouth, wraps her other hand around a lock of my hair, and lays her head down at the base of my neck.

HOME. LAND. SECURITY. SINCE OUR TOWN IS AT THE END OF AN obscure county road, since we live a mile or so south of town, and since we are the last house on this street where our backyard morphs into thousands of acres of greenbelt and wild federal land, I tell friends that our neighborhood is one of the most remote subdivisions in the lower forty-eight.

Once, while we were gone, a black bear broke in through a back door window and emptied the refrigerator, departing the same way he had come. We found his telltale claw marks on the window screen that he had ripped to shreds. Nearby tracks suggested a younger bear, one that we figured to be a transient since we were familiar with an older, bigger, and less outgoing bear whose tracks we often saw nearby and who I had once seen from a distance. Breaking and entering bears are an increasingly common occurrence along the edge of the Sangres (and elsewhere around the state), even in some cases for those who have, as we had, taken many of the usual precautions—removing bird feeders, stowing away backyard grills, sequestering trash, etcetera.

We live in an odd interface of residential neighborhood and back of beyond. If this is the "stupid zone" as *Denver Post* columnist Ed Quillen liked to say of those places that are more prone to fire and other upcountry hazards, it is one that we came to knowingly, willing to throw the dice as it were, in exchange for the kind of back yard wildness that only public lands can provide those for whom the privilege of large land holdings is not an option.

Our home is a house in a neighborhood as was my childhood home. We like to imagine Rosalea riding her bike over to a friend's house someday or maybe down to Curt's store, something Grace had never been able to do growing up on a mountain seven miles east of Mancos. When Rosalea is old enough, she may also choose to head out in the other direction, gaining a few thousand feet into wild mountain country, much as Grace might have done growing up in the La Platas.

The Baca Grande, as this settlement south of Crestone is known, is the remnant of a development scheme hatched by real estate boosters back in the 1970s. For a while they made a living selling slivers of the Rockies, sight unseen, to homesick military guys stationed in places like Guam. But eventually their venture went belly up. It has since been reinvented as a kind of mecca for various misfits, mystics, mountain folk, artists, and retirees. As suggested by the local architecture—domes, earthships, straw bale homes, and any number of variations on active and passive solar—this place is an eclectic and eccentric alternative to the usual subdivision and most everything else one might think of as mainstream.

What images of this place, this home will Rosalea carry into her later life? I can remember climbing a big pine tree out behind the house where I grew up. The sap-covered branches on that old pine were as easy to climb as the rungs on a ladder. Near the top of the tree, where the trunk grew thin enough to bend in a strong wind, I could see the top of the tower down at St. Patrick's Cathedral. Other than that occasional high glimpse into our surburban town, I didn't think much about our local geography.

Maybe every parent wants their kid to have something they have not had. I want to help create for Rosalea a home that may later be thought of as sanctuary or refuge. I want her to know this place—its rocks and trees, its birds and flowers—in ways that I never really knew my own home. That kind of familiarity is the beginning of a bonding to place that has given Grace a sure-footed way of moving out into the world. When my parents chose to sell our childhood home, I wasn't unhappy. Our bonds with that suburban home had never grown strong. But Grace still has that material link with her home place and therefore with her own beginnings. She dreams often of her childhood home and she can go there in real time as well. I want that for Rosalea.

And yet, I also know that images of home are far from static. Rosalea's vantage point and therefore her experience of this place have already changed. She has moved on from riding in the sling—close enough to my chest to hear my heartbeat—to riding in the pack on my back. The first day she rode behind me as we walked, is one of many thresholds she will cross between this time, this place, this home, and the inevitable urge she will have for leaving it. It was the first step, I imagined, on that path toward a driver's license and the road headed west out of town.

A few months after her transition to the pack, I push her in a stroller around the road that loops down through our neighborhood. The moon is out. Its light flickers across ice crystals in the snow. "I can reach the moon," Rosalea says, stretching out one of her arms.

Her imagination, as much as any other factor, will transform her orientation to this place, this home, and this world over time. Inward worlds of the imagination and the objective world "out there" are both a part of her life's (of any life's) collaborative unfolding.

Looking out from our perch on the flanks of the Sangre de

Cristos as I wheel her down our street, I can see the San Juan Mountains, some fifty miles or so off in the distance across the San Luis Valley. Given the width of our valley—eighty miles across in places—the night time optics are such that lights scattered here and there out toward the San Juans, seem to line up as if on a distant coast, not unlike the views I once saw as a kid looking out across the Long Island Sound toward Connecticut. Sometimes driving into the trees on the edge of this big valley is like sailing a small boat home to a once-known harbor.

HOME. LAND. SECURITY. TOO MUCH SECURITY CAN STIFLE THE SOUL. At least, that's what the Buddha seemed to think, having abandoned privilege and palace for a better look at the world. Jesus and his disciples, who had exchanged their homes and their vocations for the road and for "the way," also seemed to be moving away from any security they had known.

"For religions, home in its deepest sense ultimately means mystery," writes theologian John Haught. "Religions require for the sake of religious authenticity that our lives not be embedded too comfortably in any domain short of the inexhaustible mystery that is the ultimate goal and horizon of our existence."

"What about the here and now?" I wonder. "What about home and place?"

Haught asks similar questions: "Can we interpret religious homelessness in such a way as to foster a sense of being at home in the natural world?" Having posed the question, he goes on to seek out an answer. And he finds a way to respond to his query from the perspectives of cosmology and evolution.

The universe itself is restless, he reasons. As near as we can tell, it is still expanding. And we can see that life seems to be moving, here on our little piece of the rock anyway, in the direction, biologically speaking, of more and more complexity. If we think of ourselves and our religious stories as yet another expression of that evolutionary and cosmological pilgrimage, he wonders, might we not be more at home in a world that is fundamentally on the move?

My story, your story, stories read in the Bible, and the ecological story in which human lives are all embedded, are all part of the Big Story moving forward. It is an adventure that is fundamentally wild, which is to say that it is an adventure into the unknown.

"The restlessness that launched matter on its pilgrimage toward complexity twenty billion years ago has apparently not been quieted," he writes. "It continues now in our questioning minds and our spirit of exploration."

In thinking about the relationship between the longing for home and that inward restlessness that encourages movement toward a spiritual center, I am reminded of the dust and the breath in Genesis 2. In that story, the human soul is made from the dust of the ground which is then infused with God's breath. The dust of the ground and the breath of life aren't understood as separate parts. They are as intertwined as the strands of a DNA molecule. Rather than seeing the dust of the ground and the breath of life as being in relationship, we have come to understand them as separate, maybe even opposed to one another.

The same can be said of our relationship with place: we have come to see ground and Spirit (from the Latin "spirer"—to breathe) as separate entities. That which might be gleaned from Genesis 2, from cosmology and evolution, and from a little girl's sense of wonder on the flanks of the Sangre de Cristos, questions that view. What if we understood place and Spirit as akin, respectively, to the dust and the breath? What if the need for home (dust) and that restless spirit (breath), which leads one further into the Great Mystery, were both understood as elemental and interrelated on the human pilgrimage?

Home. Land. Security. Around our house, some of the biggest pinyon and juniper trees I've ever seen offer us a little shelter from the wind and weather that often blows in hard from the southwest. Nearby, a little to our south, a line of aspens that follows Crestone Creek down the mountain adds to our sense of enclosure and harbors warblers and western tanagers during the warmer months, as well as a colony of turkey vultures.

In the mornings, the vultures leave their nearby roost, drifting down along the line of aspens then cottonwoods that follow the mountain drainages out onto the valley floor, scanning county roads with eye and nose for the latest roadkill. In the evenings, we watch them come home to our perch on the flanks of the Sangres, circling by overhead and spiraling down to their roost in the aspens along Crestone Creek, about a quarter of a mile to our south. The arroyo they often seem to follow to and from their roost runs by our house. In their honor, we call it Vulture Gulch.

One morning, I entice Rosalea into the pack with the prospect of a visit to the vulture roost down the road. It is early enough in the morning that few of them have left. As we follow the trail along the creek into a little clearing, we see them overhead, at least twenty vultures, several of them facing toward the sun, their wings outspread and gathering sunlight.

"Don't disturb them, Papa," Rosalea says, after a minute or two looking up at them in that clearing. We keep walking. Down the trail, several vultures fly overhead

"Where do you think they're going?" I ask Rosalea.

"They're going to school church," she says.

"Where's that?"

"It's way out there," she says, pointing out over the valley. "And it's where your dreams go when you close your eyes."

Acknowledgments

For the mountain places that have given me refuge and a place to learn: the High Uintas, the Sangre de Cristos, the Wasatch Range, the Sawatch Range, the La Plata Range and the Henry Mountains. Without wild places, I would have little to say.

For all the family support over the years. For tolerant, patient, and loving parents and a sister who has been great company on many roads and trails. For grandparents who suggested I write and helped me to do so.

For all the great writing mentors over the years—Dick Davis (College of the Atlantic), Red Bird and David Peterson (Fort Lewis College), Robert Roripaugh (University of Wyoming), Tom Mullen and Paul Lacey (Earlham School of Religion), John Tallmadge (Union Institute), Pat Schneider (Amherst Writers and Artists).

For the many friends and teachers, especially at Earlham School of Religion, who took the time to read drafts of various chapters. For their honest critiques and encouragment along the way.

For Friends at Salt Lake Monthly Meeting who helped me find the stillness in Quaker worship.

For the community of mentors and seekers at Earlham School of Religion who helped me to find the way forward. And for the members of Clear Creek and First Friends who welcomed us into heir meetings for worship.

For financial support from the Utah Arts Council, the Cooper Scholarship at Earlham School of Religion, the Patrick Henry Writng Fellowship, and a New Voices Essay Award from the Institute of Ecumenical and Cultural Research.

For Caleb Seeling, Sonya Unrein and their support for this project.

For a great circle of friends who have offered me their encouragement and support along the way.

For a lovely and patient wife who loves mountains as much as I do and for two lovely daughters whose genes leave them little choice.

I am truly thankful.

—Peter Anderson, Vulture Gulch
Crestone, Colorado, November, 2014